Locked Up
and
Locked Down

Locked Up and Locked Down

Multitude Lingers in Limbo

George Walters-Sleyon

Copyright © 2010 by George Walters-Sleyon.

Library of Congress Control Number:		2009901460
ISBN:	Hardcover	978-1-4415-1200-0
	Softcover	978-1-4415-1199-7

All rights reserved. No part of this book may be reproduced or transmitted in any form or by any means, electronic or mechanical, including photocopying, recording, or by any information storage and retrieval system, without permission in writing from the copyright owner.

This book was printed in the United States of America.

To order additional copies of this book, contact:
Xlibris Corporation
1-888-795-4274
www.Xlibris.com
Orders@Xlibris.com

Prayer

Shine on us and enlighten our sight
Shine on us and blight our slums
Shine on us and lighten our sigh
Shine on us and slice our slumber
Enlighten our sight to behold your emblem
Blight our slums to bespeak our humanity
Lighten our sigh to beget your humility
Slice our slumber to bestow our empathy
For in your emblem we are restored
In our humanity we are renewed
In your humility we are returned
In our empathy we are resigned

(George Walters-Sleyon)

Contents

Foreword		13
Introduction		15
	Reading G. W. F. Hegel	16
Chapter One:	**My Story**	25
Chapter Two:	**The "Situation"**	41
	The Imprisoned Black Man	48
	The Why Factor	53
	Social Consequences	62
	Imprisonment Is Not a Rite of Passage	67
	Crime and Persecution	
Chapter Three	**What Does the Bible Say?**	76
Chapter Four	**Am I Worthy as I Am?**	88
Chapter Five	**A Call to the Black Church**	111
Chapter Six	**What Do We Do?**	120
	A Prophetic Response	121
	A Rational Response	128
	A Critical Response	134
	A Pragmatic Response	137
Prayer		141
Appendix		143
Bibliography		147
Index		157

Dedicated to Mama Annie

Who "introduced" me to God and Papa Andrew Mitten-Sleyon-Wreh Walters

Who introduced me to reading.

Mama lives in West Point/Monrovia Liberia and Papa lives in heaven.

But your Balluu loves you.

My Mother, My Father

You love me and I know it

I love you and will always love you.

Acknowledgement

The demand of writing this book would have been impossible without the help of friends, relatives, professors, clergymen and praying mothers. I owe a debt of gratitude to Dr. Darlingston Johnson of the Bethel World Outreach Ministries in Silver Spring, Maryland, Dr. Mensah Otabil of the International Central Gospel Church in Ghana, my Boston University School of Theology family and the friends of the New England Annual Conference of the United Methodist Church. My special thanks go to Dr. Fred Allen, Bishop Peter Weaver, Rev. Lawrence Wimmer, Rev. Aida Fernandez, Rev. Bernard Alex, and Rod Foqua and my brothers: Dr. Glenn W. W. Moore and Philip Sleyon. I thank my advisors: Dr. John Hart, Dr. Norman Faramelli, Dr. Garth Green and Dr. Dale Andrews for their continuous intellectual support. Special thanks to my friends, especially Miss. Velma DuPont for her editorial support. And finally, my deepest gratitude is to God in the name of Jesus Christ who set me free. Peace and rest to all who read these words.

Foreword

By Rodney L. Petersen, PhD

Executive Director, Boston Theological Institute

Locked Up and Locked Down focuses on one of the most profound anomalies of the twenty-first century, that the nation that most trumpets freedom and democracy is also the one with the highest rate of incarceration: One in 100 Americans is in prison or jail at the time of the publication of this book. The United States leads the world in both the number and percentage of residents it incarcerates.

Even more scandalous is the racial disparity that accompanies these numbers, that one in nine black men ages 20 to 34 is behind bars; and for black women ages 35 to 39, the figure is one in 100, compared with one in 355 for white women in the same age group. This raises the obvious question: why is there such a disparity?

Many experts attribute the increase in America's prison population to tougher sentencing. For example, the famous "three strikes" rule has led to an increase in the time people spend in prison. Then, too, there are the cycles of violence that more overtly accompany economic depravation and social disadvantage and lead to the asocial behavior dealt with through the criminal justice system.

Yet, it is ironic that at just the time that America celebrates a person of African-American heritage in the White House, we are drawn in this study to a continuing racism that shapes the underlying factors behind elevated rates of incarceration.

The historical conditions that compound this racism have social ramifications that perpetuate it, a story that is well told by Orlando Patterson in *Rituals of Blood: The Consequences of Slavery in Two American Centuries*. Walters-Sleyon picks up the thread and draws us to prison as rite of passage for many young men and as surrogate welfare for a failed social policy. Drawing upon the insightful work of Christopher Marshall, he shows how all of this is at variance from a guiding biblical vision as well as from the intent in the founding of prisons as places of moral and social rehabilitation.

Writing for church and academy alike, Walters-Sleyon draws us through his own story of imprisonment to conceptions of the dignity and rights that come into play in the courtroom. For example, against a philosophy of the right laid out by G. W. F. Hegel that finds a criminal still to be a criminal even when he has been punished and freed, Walters-Sleyon points to the biblical vision and Augustinian theological tradition for a liberating and restorative understanding of the human person, a view taken up by Pope John Paul II.

While acknowledging that incarceration is appropriate for crime, Walters-Sleyon targets arbitrary arrest, racially motivated sentencing, the criminalization of black men and their commodification by a growing commercial prison industrial complex in a study that easily traverses the worlds of theory and practice. Following the guidance of *The Covenant with Black America*, Walters-Sleyon concludes with practical steps for churches and civic organizations that are prophetic, rational, critical, and pragmatic.

Introduction

My aim in this book is to present a theological and existential analysis of the high rate of detention and incarceration of black men in the prison system in America. I believe the disparity evident in the increasing rates of incarceration and detention of black men serves as the most powerful form of disempowerment for the black man today. There are over one million black men detained and incarcerated comprising over half of the 2.4 million people detained and incarcerated in prisons around the USA. The social implications are negatively impacting, the economic consequence is generational and the health consequences of HIV and AIDS demand immediate response. This book is also a narrative that seeks to analyze the assumptions that enforce the lenses through which the black man is perceived as a criminal. Within the context of a theological and biblical analysis, I want to assert that the criminal is not inherently a criminal. Apart from personal causes, this book argues that there are fundamental sociopolitical and economic factors informed by the consciousness of the society that ought to be taken into consideration if one is to understand the criminal, his crime, and his criminality.

Ultimately, my goal in presenting this work is to appeal to the Body of Christ. In directing this work to the Body of Christ, I am attempting to highlight the awareness that the absence of the Church to mount a concerted effort in responding to the dilemma of the high rate of detained and incarcerated black men as a result of the implications of the activities of the commercial prison—industrial complex is troublesome. The Church is called upon in this time to respond to the plight of over one million imprisoned black men as a result of a prophetic necessity. I believe the high rates of incarceration and detention of black men is the number one social problem facing the Church in the 21st century. God is calling upon the Church in America to respond deliberately and intentionally, and not to turn away from this problem. This book will accomplish its goals if it is able to spur the Church to see the need for a transformative response and intervention to the existential and social implications of over 1.3 million black men behind bars. To avoid addressing the issue of the increasing rates of incarcerated and detained black men will become an even greater travesty since silence is the best weapon for normalizing a precarious situation, and insensitivity is its advocate.

This research began as a result of a political philosophy course I was enrolled in during the spring of 2007. The course was on G. W. F. Hegel and the main text was *Elements of the Philosophy of Right.* In Hegel's view on crime and punishment, I saw a notion of inherent criminality that stigmatizes the criminal and criminalizes anyone who commits crime, thus resonating with a prevailing notion of crime especially as it relates to black men in America and the disparity evident in the high rates of detained and incarcerated black men in the prison system. I became interested in Hegel's views of crime and punishment in light of the criminalization of black men, the high rate of incarcerated and detained black men and the activities of what is called the commercial prison—industrial complex. I was curious about the link between the increase in the prison-industrial complex and the stigmatization of black men as criminals, the social implications for black boys, and the black family structure. As a minister, I wanted to search for a biblical response that could be derived by delving into this kind of analysis. While I do not see racism in every punishment meted out against crime committed by black men, I am equally sensitive to the present rate of incarceration and detention of black men and boys in the prison system as a person who preaches the Word of God. I believe God is grieved by the high rate of detained and incarcerated black men fundamentally influenced by economic gains on the part of the commercial prison—industrial complex in the United States today.

The book was conceived both academically and personally as a preacher. It is intended for both audiences, especially the latter. This being the case, the book includes some of the rigors of the academic reflection but since it is intended for a broad audience it does not explore the details of academic technicalities at length. This is especially true of the Hegel's section which involves subtle distinctions on abstract and concrete right, individual right and state right, retribution etc. The figures whose works are referenced in this book are referenced to underscore their existential and theological importance to the overall narrative that I am attempting to share. My attempt is not to enter into the academic debate of their works but simply to emphasize the portions of their works that convey their identity with human suffering and alienation. In that light, this book is also an attempt to present an existential analysis of the plight of over one million incarcerated and detained black men.

Structurally, the book is divided into three sections. Section 1 is descriptive: chapters 1 and 2 provide a descriptive analysis of the high rate of incarceration and detention and the fundamental sociopolitical consciousness informing the statistical increase. Section 2 is mainly analytical: In chapters 3 and 4, I provide a theological analysis of chapters 1 and 2 and a theological critique of racial consciousness. This section also establishes the argument that the person is an ontological being of inherent worth, possessing the "spark of God" in them (and to reduce that inherent worth of divine dignity to inherent criminality as society has identified some is a violation of the image of God in every human being). Crime is not "infinite," this section argues, and the criminal is not an inherent criminal. The theological analysis also provides critique of the prevailing social anthropology by asserting a biblical and theological understanding of the human person beyond the characterizations of race, racism, and racialization as fundamental lenses through which justice is executed. Section 3 is prescriptive; in chapters 5 and 6, I provide an analysis of the role of the Black Church. Section 3 concludes with suggestions that also provide internal critique of the black community. It calls on us to adopt measures necessary for adequate change and transformation.

Footnote: An academic discussion of these terms would have to weigh how I argue concerning the indelible image of God and how it is conceived on the basis of a different definition of right as "we hold these truths to be self-evident, that all men are created equal." One would have to explore Hegel's notion of right vis-à-vis the liberal democratic notion of right that is our standard understanding of right, that is, the natural, indelible constitution of every person.

Reading G. W. F. Hegel:

> *"The United States Has by far the world's highest incarceration rate. With 5% of the world's population, our country now houses nearly 25% of the world's reported prisoners. We currently incarcerate 756 inmates per 100,000 residents, a rate nearly five times the average worldwide of 158 for every 100,000. In addition, more than 5 million people who recently left jail remain under 'correctional supervision,' which includes parole, probation, and other community sanctions. All told, about one in every 31 adults in the United States is in prison, in jail, or on supervised release . . . Either we are home to the most evil people on earth or we are doing something different . . ."*

Senator Jim Wibb, *What's Wrong With Our Prisons?*
Boston Sunday Globe-Parade, p.4

Hegel's *Element of the Philosophy of Right* is fundamentally a part of his entire philosophical system. It reflects a systematic development of the concept of "right" as it develops into an "idea of right." Interestingly, while Hegel's *Philosophy of Right* is highly conceptual and theoretical, one cannot help but notice the influence of his theory in the formulation of policies regarding the sentencing of criminals in the 21st century.

What struck me the most, among the many interpretations of Hegel's view of crime and punishment—whether as a retributivist, a semiretributivist, or a nonretributivist—were two dominant claims embedded in his theory regarding the criminal: first, that the criminal is still a criminal even when he has been punished and freed, and secondly, that the criminal is still a criminal even when pardoned and granted executive clemency by the sovereign. The criminal by committing a crime has lost his right. Only God can effectively pardon a criminal in the realm of the spirit, but in the concrete world of sociopolitical and economic activities, the criminal will remain a criminal and will always be viewed as a criminal. According to Hegel's argument, pardon is the remission of punishment, but it is not a cancellation of right (the right to meet crime with crime). On the contrary, right continues to apply, and the pardoned individual still remains a criminal; the pardon does not state that he has not committed a crime. This cancellation [*Aufhebung*] of punishment may be effected by religion, for what has been done can only be undone in the spirit by the spirit itself. But in so far as it is accomplished in this world, it is to be found only in the majesty [of the sovereign] and is the prerogative of [the sovereign's] ungrounded decision.[1] According to the above, the criminal will always be a criminal even after his or her punishment. To better understand Hegel's argument in this context, one must understand his notion of right in relation to crime and punishment.

Hegel believes that every individual has what he calls "abstract right,"[2] which indicates their inherent claim to individual right manifested through the will of the individual in the world.[3] Right is first an abstract entity and secondarily a concrete entity. *Right* implies the will of the individual to himself as purely a subjective person. Since every individual has abstract right, which also becomes concrete in the world, Hegel says every individual must exist according to the commandment of right, i.e., "Be a person and respect others as persons."[4] On the other hand, that right can be taken away when a person commits a criminal act since "crime in itself is an infinite injury."[5] Crime is an infinite injury not only with respect to the jury done to the victim of the crime but to the criminal himself, i.e., crime as an infinite injury affects the abstract right of the criminal apart from his concrete right in the world. That is why the criminal will be perpetually stigmatized as a criminal even when he has paid the due penalty for his crime.

---

1. G. W. F. Hegel, *Element of the Philosophy of Right* (Ed. Allen Wood, Cambridge University, 1991), PR. 282, (see: PR. 97A, 99) *Aufheben* for Hegel in English implies "Sublation." It means to "preserve", to maintain and also to "cause to cease" i.e. to "put to an end" (See: *The Science of Logic*, Pp. 45, 46, 107).

2. Ibid., PR, 2, 19.

3. Ibid. PR. 4

4. Ibid., PR. 36.

5. Ibid., PR. 218, "Crime *in itself* is an infinite injury, but as an *existence* [*Dasein*], it must be measured in terms of qualitative and quantitative differences and since its existence is essentially determined as a *representation* [*Vorstellung*] and *consciousness of the validity of the laws,* its *danger to civil society* is a determination of its magnitude, or even *one* of its qualitative determinations."

"Crime" as the most grievous of wrongs takes away the right of the one who commits it.[6] Since the individual's right is primarily internal and secondarily external in the real world, when crime is committed, it reflects the implementation of the doer's abstract right and will in the real world. Because crime is an infringement of right, and right cannot be cancelled, crime must be cancelled by right in the form of punishment. Hegel argues that "the criminal act . . . is itself negative, so that the punishment is merely the negation of the negation. Actual right is thus the cancellation [*Aufhebung*] of this infringement . . ."[7] The right to commit a crime can only be punished by the right to punish crime. Therefore, right must punish right and right must prevail, i.e., the right of the state must punish the right of the criminal, thereby taking away the right of the criminal. The criminal is still a citizen but a rightless citizen whose right has been taken away by the state.

Since crime implies the negation of right, the punishment must be in proportion to the crime committed because punishment implies the negation of crime on the part of right. According to Hegel, punishment is the state's right punishing the criminal's right for committing crime. The implication is that punishment does not only affect the will of the criminal in the world but also affects the abstract right of the criminal. Crime is both physical and spiritual. It also implies that the criminal is spiritually a criminal first before they concretely committed the

---

6. Ibid., PR. 86, 87, 88, 95.

7. Ibid., PR. 97. "Through a crime, something is altered, and the thing [*Sache*] exists in this alteration; but this existence is the opposite of thing itself, and is to that extent within itself [*in sich*] null and void. The nullity is [the presumption] that right as right has been cancelled [*aufgehoben*]. For right, as an absolute, cannot be cancelled, so that the expression of crime is within itself null and void, and this nullity is the essence of the effect of crime. But whatever is null and void must manifest itself as such that is, it must itself appear as vulnerable. The criminal act is not an initial positive occurrence followed by the punishment as its negation, but is itself negative, so that the punishment is merely the negation of the negation. Actual right is thus the cancellation [*Aufhebung*] of this infringement, and it is in this very circumstance that it demonstrates its validity and proves itself as a necessary and mediated existence [*Dasein*]."

LOCKED UP AND LOCKED DOWN

crime. That is why the sovereign can only pardon the criminal from punishment in the world but cannot pardon the criminal based on abstract right.[8] In summary, the punishment meted out against the criminal does not only affect the will of the criminal but also affects his or her abstract right as well.

Hegel argues that the act of the criminal reflects his will; therefore, any punishment incompatible with the crime committed reflects the dishonoring of the criminal. "The action of the criminal involves not only the *concept* of crime [but] its rationality *in and for itself* which the state must enforce *with or without* the consent of individual's [*der Einzelnen*] volition."[9] Since the crime involved reflects the will of the criminal, his consent to be punished is entailed within the crime committed. His consent is no longer needed when he stands before the judge because his crime, which expresses his will, takes away any recognition of his abstract right, will, or freedom in the concrete world. Of course, the criminal must be punished. According to Hegel, the criminal is "honored" if he is not consulted with respect to his punishment since he has already committed a crime that is the expression of his will and right. Hegel argues, "that the punishment which this entails is seen as embodying the criminal's own right," therefore, he is honored. But he is dishonored "if the concept and criterion of his punishment are not derived from his own act; and he is also denied it if he is regarded simply as a harmful animal which must be rendered harmless, or punished with a view to deterring or reforming him."[10] When the criminal is punished with a punishment proportional to his action, he is

---

8.   Ibid., PR. 100: According to Hegel: "The injury [*Verletzung*] which is inflicted on the criminal is not only just *in itself* (and since it is just, it is at the same time his will as it is in *itself,* an existence [*Dasein*] of his freedom, *his* right); it is also a right *for the criminal himself,* that is, a right *posited* in his *existent* will, in his action. For it is implicit in his action, as that of a *rational* being, that it is universal in character, and that by performing it, he has set up a law which he has recognized for himself in his action, and under which he may therefore be subsumed as under *his* right."

9.   Ibid., PR. 100,

10.   Ibid., PR. 100,

honored as a rational being, and his rational will is fully recognized. To refuse to punish in proportion to his crime is to dishonor him. Punishment is not a deterrent; it is not restorative, rehabilitative, or transformative. For Hegel, crime is a legal transfer of right to the state; therefore, punishment, i.e., imprisonment, is a necessary measure to effect the taking away of the right of the criminal, and criminalization is the means to enforce the taking away of such right. For Hegel, "The criminal gives his consent by his very act" to be punished.[11] But one should note that Hegel does not support "reforming" the criminal. In this light, reforming the criminal so as to prevent future crime is not the issue of priority in Hegel's analysis of crime and punishment.

The role of punishment is to cancel the crime committed since the crime committed is an act of the will of the criminal. Punishment is executed against the will of the criminal to cancel the crime committed. Therefore, the only right the criminal has even after his imprisonment is one that is criminally influenced. To reiterate, the sovereign can only pardon the criminal from being punished physically but not pardoned, his abstract will is now criminalized.[12] In that light, the criminal will always be a criminal. Based on the above, only God can totally pardon a criminal in the realm of the spirit, but in this concrete world of human activities, the criminal must be viewed as a criminal and "rightless" in the society even when pardoned by the sovereign of the state.

---

11.   Ibid., PR. 100, 101. "Both the nature of the crime and the criminal's own will require that the infringement for which he is responsible should be cancelled [*aufgehoben*] .... The cancellation [*Aufheben*] of crime is *retribution* in so far as the latter, by its concept, is an infringement of an infringement, and in so far as crime, by its existence [*Dasein*], has a determinate qualitative and quantitative magnitude, so that its negation, as existent, also has a determinate magnitude."

12.   Ibid., PR. 101, pg. 128 "Yet the concept itself must always contain the basic principle, even for the particular instance. This determination of the concept, however, is precisely that necessary connection [which dictates] that crime, as the will which is null and void in itself, accordingly contains within itself its own nullification, and this appears in the form of punishment."

With this insight, it is not difficult to see how Hegel's notion of crime and punishment can be detrimental for some, since it legitimizes a perpetual criminalization of the criminal. The criminal is rightless. He is a citizen, but unlike other citizens, he is rightless. With the above analysis, I have attempted to analyze the socioeconomic condition of over one million black men in prison and out of prisons as "rightless" men within the context of Hegel's views on crime and punishment. Hegel's enlightenment views and the conceptual development of his theory on crime and punishment is very problematic. It perpetuates a consciousness of "criminalization" rather than advance cogent solutions for "decriminalization." This suspicion is especially poignant when we take into consideration the history of colonialism, imperialism, tribalism, slavery, racism, and discrimination that have informed our modern consciousness of justice, public policy formulation, international relations, and sociopolitical and economic activities. Yet little did I know that my research was going to be experiential and firsthand. This book is also a story about my five-day detention at a Federal Detention Facility in March of 2008 after I began my personal research in February of 2007.

But it was in detention that I discovered another missing link in my research: the relationship between the high detention rate of African and African Caribbean immigrants for deportation in detention facilities and the high rate of incarcerated African Americans men across the United States in contrast to every other nationality or ethnic group.

This work is an integration of theology and social justice. It is devotional and seeks to bring inspiration and information to whoever reads it: renewed insight and conviction to the church leader and student. But it is also an existential analysis. I want to capture in words the anguish, agony, and despair associated with the disproportion evident in the high rate of detention and incarceration of black men. It seeks to translate into words the feeling of self-negation and distortion that such experiences often engender. I believe beneath the crucibles of political strength, economic empowerment, and social stability resides the realities of despair, dismay, and desperation for survival. In its harsh reality, the economically and socially marginalized, the detained, incarcerated, and abandoned scream for help and, in their anguish, are forced to question their existence, their sense of being, and their sense of worth.[13] To reiterate my argument, I do not believe the criminal is inherently a criminal, apart from personal causes. There are sociopolitical and economic factors that need to be considered in light of the sentencing policies and the economic activities of the prison-industrial complex. What will Hegel say about racial preference in the sentence process affecting thousands of black men? How will Hegel's system respond to historical assumptions and consciousness that criminalizes one group of people? How will his system respond to what has now become a multibillion dollar industry: the prison-industrial complex in the United States fundamentally fed by race, poverty, illiteracy, and less by "crime"?

As a preacher, I see some of the best solutions emerging from the Body of Christ, the Black Church, and the Missionary churches. The Church is able to bring into reality a kind of transformation that can only be achieved by working with individuals who have come to understand the shared mutuality of human connectedness: one that transcends race, creed, and color.

[13.] Ben Campbell Johnson, *Rethinking Evangelism: A Theological Approach* (Philadelphia, The Westminister Press, 1987) 32 "Where did I come from? (Sense of origin), Who am I? (Sense of identity), What is wrong with me? (Sense of alienation), Why am I here? (Sense of meaning) and Where am I going? (Sense of destiny)."

Chapter One

My Story

"Because he loves me," says the Lord, "I will rescue him, I will protect him, for he acknowledges my name. He will call upon me, and I will answer him; I will be with him in trouble, I will deliver him and honor. With long life will I satisfy him and show him my salvation."

—Psalm 90:14-16

It was five o'clock in the morning; a friend dropped me off at the Greyhound bus station in Syracuse, New York. I was on my way to Toledo University in Ohio to attend a conference as a presenter and a guest artist. The date was March 27, 2008. We said good-bye, and my car was driven back to the house. The conference was scheduled for March 28-29.

I was invited to present a paper on *Postwar Reconstruction and Ethical Imagination* and, as a gospel recording artist, to also serve as a guest singer. I was excited, and with much anticipation, I looked forward to the conference. It was the highlight of my academic training at the time.

I boarded the Greyhound bus at 6:30 a.m. The bus was scheduled to make a quick stop in Rochester, New York before moving on to

Buffalo where I was scheduled to change buses to Cleveland and finally to Columbus, Ohio, my final stop.

Between Syracuse and Buffalo, I decided to take a nap. I had been up since 3:00 a.m. packing my bags. I woke up just before we reached Rochester for our quick stop. We arrived in Rochester at around 8:30 a.m. Some people got off the bus and others came on. But just before we could continue, two border patrol officers got on board and asked to see our identification cards. One came directly over to me, sat on the seat next to me, and asked to see my identification card. I took out my Massachusetts driver's license and my Boston University student identification card. He went to the back of the bus to inspect them.

After inspecting my cards, he returned and sat next to me again. This time, he said his record indicated that I had traveled in 2005 and 2007 to Canada and Mexico respectively and that he was going to arrest me. Before I could respond, he interrupted and said that I had overstayed my student visa. Again, before I could tell him that I had never traveled out of this country since I arrived, that I was not even on a student visa, and that I have been a student at Boston University since 2001. I informed him that I was a United Methodist clergyman, and that I was on my way to attend a conference at the University of Toledo in Ohio where I was scheduled to speak and sing, but he cut me off with the threat of arrest. To my dismay, shame, and humiliation, and as everyone on the bus listened and stared at me, he asked me to get off the bus and he arrested me. Hastily, my Greyhound ticket was returned to me, and my luggage was taken off the bus. I was transported in the patrol car to the patrol office in Rochester, utterly shocked. My mind raced faster than I knew it could as I processed my current reality, an abysmal reality.

As we entered the patrol office in Rochester, I noticed an assortment of suitcases and bags bundled upon one another in the corner. There must have been over a hundred suitcases and bags. At the office, I was processed, and a bond was set. As I sat there wondering what was going to happen next, the officer told me to find someone to come and collect my bags. He said he was taking me to the Federal Detention Facility, and if no one came to get my bags after two weeks, they would be placed among the assortment of bags and suitcases I had noticed in the left-hand corner upon entering the building. Thereafter, my bags together with the others would be trashed. I shuddered at the thought of my bags being trashed, and at the thought of the rest of the suitcases and bags in their different shapes and colors being trashed. I frantically tried to think of someone who could travel to Rochester and collect my bags. One of the bags had my CDs, and the other, my suits, purchased on a tight student budget. I could not bear the thought of losing them. I began to call my fellow pastors, friends, and relatives to tell them what was happening to me and where I was. I had no idea what was actually awaiting me.

As I sat in the office, I saw the border patrol officers bring in more people arrested off the Greyhound buses and Amtrak train. They were all black men, except for a Jamaican woman with two kids, and she was pregnant. The kids wandered around the room playing and to the annoyance of the officers, they were placed behind bars as the officers interrogated the mother who by now was on the verge of tears as her children screamed for their mama and papa from behind the bars. She knew she was not illegal as her husband had her papers but fright and shock prevented her from providing the right information. I saw a fellow with a video camera taping the interrogation, and at the time, I guessed he was from an organization that had some legal rights to record the arrest and the interrogation because the officers were uncomfortable with his presence. The pregnant lady and the men were processed, and their bags and suitcases taken from them. I could not help but entertain the following questions in my mind. If the officers trashed the bags and suitcases, what happened to the valuables in them? Are they simply placed in the truck, or are they opened individually, searched, valuables taken out, and the rest trashed? Who takes their valuables out of them? Is someone searching these bags and suitcases, taking the valuables out and selling them to the general public? Is someone making money off the bags of these people? Unfortunately, those released after two weeks do not get their bags and suitcases returned to them. They leave the detention facility only with the clothes in which they were arrested. They are transported to the nearest bus station, and if no one picks them up, they must begin again.

Similarly, I began to think about the fares of those taken off the Greyhound buses and Amtrak train like myself. What becomes of their money? One would think their ticket fares would be returned to them immediately for the rest of the journey. Unfortunately, their tickets are returned to them, but not the fares. After an arrest, the border patrol officer transports the arrestee to the border patrol building to be processed, at which time a bond is set usually in the amount of $10,000, an exorbitant amount for someone under such circumstances. They are then whisked off to the Federal Detention Facility or County Jail if the FDF is full. How will the person arrested return the ticket to retrieve his or her money? I do not know, but one thing is certain. They are placed in detention or jail and deported after seeing a judge or must linger between indefinite detention and indefinite deportation. By the time they are released if the bond is posted, Greyhound's and Amtrak's return date to receive their money back must have expired. Like the ambiguity surrounding their bags and suitcases left at the border patrol office when they were arrested, their ticket fares with Greyhound Bus and Amtrak remain with Greyhound Bus and Amtrak. I couldn't stop pondering these things. But for now, I must concentrate on my own problem and stop this wondering, I said to myself.

Pondering over my arrest in the patrol office, I repeated my claim to the officer who arrested me. I told him I have never traveled out of the United States since I arrived. To my utter dismay and with a smile on his face, he responded, "It wasn't you; it was someone else; forget it." I waited for him to say, "get your bags and let me take you back to the bus stop." But to no avail, I only heard, "forget it." "Forget it?" I repeated in my mind. I asked him if I could be released. He said no. I could not believe what I was hearing. I stood speechless. I pondered the phrase, its implication, consequences, and impact for my life: "Forget it"—he was saying, he lied in order to arrest me. "Forget it." Did he care that my life, my dreams, my hopes, and my aspirations were being shattered? Did he care that I would languish in jail if no one could come to my rescue? Did he care that I would be indefinitely in detention not knowing from one day to the next whether I would be deported? If it wasn't me, why was he so quick to arrest me? Why didn't he listen to me? Did he have to arrest me to make up his quota for the day? Was it because I am a black man and he thought I was a criminal, and someone he shouldn't waste his time listening to? I shuddered at the flippancy with which my humanity was disregarded; my destiny tossed; my dreams consigned to the wind; and my expectation for the day, the weekend, and my life trampled upon as insignificant. I wondered how many people, especially black men, he must have harmed by lying on them and telling them to "forget it" while consigning their lives to destitution and despair. I trembled within with fear and trepidation. If I am guilty, I must admit my fault, but if I am not guilty, why not listen to me? Even the guilty must be heard. I was arrested by 8:45 a.m. and held behind bars at the patrol border office. At 3:00 p.m., I was whisked off to the Federal Detention Facility. In less than twenty-four hours, I found myself frantically trying to make contact with the outside world as freedom evaded me and fright consumed me.

I first entered the United States in September of 1999. It was during the years of the civil crisis in Liberia. Liberians in the United States had being granted a legal status called temporary protective status or TPS for short, which has now been changed to deferred enforced departure. I filed for TPS immediately and was able to regularize my status. Due to the civil crisis, I could not return. My desire was to take advantage of the temporary protective status provided for Liberians and go to school. In 2001, I entered Boston University's masters of divinity program and graduated in 2004 with a master of Divinity. In the fall of 2004, I enrolled in a postgraduate masters program and graduated in 2006 with a master's degree in philosophy, theology, and ethics with a specialization in social ethics. In the same year, I was accepted into the doctoral program in philosophy, theology, and ethics—a program I am currently completing while continuing a singing ministry as a gospel artist and a preacher.

As a gospel artist, I recorded my second album with the title *Hold on You Will Survive.* The goal of the album was to capture the anguish of war in music and to support an orphanage with some of the proceeds. With the help of some friends, I rearranged some old spirituals like "Nobody Knows the Trouble I See," "His Eye Is on the Sparrow," "The Old Rugged Cross" together with some original compositions like "Am I Worthy as I Am," "Too Many a Night," "Make It to the End," "Hold on You Will Survive," etc. But all of this was about to be trampled upon and trivialized. As I sat on my bunk bed, tears rolled down my face as locking gates and closing doors sounded my demise while the darkness of the night reflected my doom. Yet deep within me I felt the sense of hope and the bubbling up of one of my favorite Psalms.

> I will lift up my eyes to the hills
> Where does my help come from
> My help comes from the Lord,
> The Maker of heaven and earth.
> He will not let my foot slip
> He who watches over me will not slumber;
> Indeed, he who watches over Israel

Will neither slumber nor sleep.
The Lord watches over me
The Lord is my shade at my right hand,
The sun will not harm me by day
Nor the moon by night.
The Lord will keep me from all harm
He will watch over my life;
The Lord will watch over my coming and my going
Both now and forevermore. (Psalm 121)

At the front desk in the detention facility, I was processed, and everything was taken away from me including my books. While being processed, my phone rang, and I noticed it was one of my pastor friends calling to inquire. As I tried to pick it up, the officer screamed at me. He said if I picked the phone up, he was going to break it. I watched it as it rang and went off. I fought back tears as they watched me. After the processing, I was stripped and given a blue suit together with two pairs of underwear, socks, pair of slippers, sheets, and toiletries. A deportation officer was assigned to me. My cell phone and all other belongings were taken away. The only personal belongings I was allowed to keep were my Bible and my glasses. I was assigned to a unit, and a bunk bed was given to me. It was after 8:00 p.m. I was exhausted, and sleep would not allow me to stay awake.

I woke up at six the next morning, and I didn't want to open my eyes. I knew where I was. I was tangibly in detention and was not having a dream. Depressed and frustrated, I began to pray and ask God what was happening. It was then that I heard a still small voice saying to me, "Remember you have been working on this; look around you and see." It was surreal, but it was real. I "opened" my eyes. A part of me wanted to deny it, but my surroundings reminded me. The bunk bed that I was sleeping on, the blanket I was covered with, the blue suits that had now become my identity, the slippers, the black-and-white sneakers, the tiny toothbrush that refused to clean the middle and end of my entire mouth, but only scanned it while leaving my teeth painfully brushed and my fingers painfully bruised because of its bewildering length; not forgetting the despairing eyes that gazed in their uncertainty. Something within me said, "you are in lock-up; get used to it." But I knew I could not get used to it. Since my teenage years, I have uncannily believed that my life had a purpose, that God was with me in ways unexplainable and that God's plan for my life could not be thwarted. In my life I search for God in every situation and I have not been abandoned. This was not my end, I whispered and assured myself.

At breakfast I got to see all the other detainees of my unit. I noticed more men from Africa and the Caribbean than Latinos, Caucasians, or Arabs. I became curious. I wanted to hear their stories. I began to initiate some friendship. I sat at a table with three other detainees. We introduced ourselves since I was the newest one there. I told them that I was from Liberia, and I had just come the day before. One was an elderly gentleman. I noticed he was eating a different diet from the one the rest of us were served. He introduced himself and said he was from Nigeria. He had a special diet because he was diabetic. The fellow on my right was from Guinea. He was a musician. He was arrested in Rochester during the '07 Christmas holidays on his way to a program and family gathering. The fellow on my left was from Mali. He was the youngest and was looking very depressed. He ate less and less of his food. There was another fellow from another African country; four of us were from West Africa. We became friends, and for as long as I was there, we ate together. But I also later realized that my unit was not the only one filled with Africans or Caribbeans. There were two major halls for immigrants; most of the occupants were Africans and Caribbeans. I met some of them on the second day when we went outside in the yard to walk. There were older men and young men. I discovered that they came from the four regions of Africa: West, North, East, and South Africa. They wore blues suits and brown jackets like us. One day we got to talking about Africa. The conversation was very informative and intellectual. They spoke English very well, and there was a level of intellectual awareness that could not be denied. Through the conversation, I got to know that many of them had acquired postsecondary and college education before coming to the United States. They regretted where they were and felt their lives were being wasted. This was not their impression of America—only if they had remained in Africa, they said. But the saddest part about their being in there was that most of their relatives in Africa and the United States had little or no clue as to what had happened to them. Some of them had been taken off the Greyhound buses or Amtrak train and by now, had little contact with relatives and friends. They had depleted the little money they were arrested with. Their families in Africa only know that their children and relatives are in America; as to their present condition, most families are unaware. It was then that I also began to understand why most families in Africa who have relatives and children in the United States and other parts of Europe sometimes complain that they don't hear from their children and relatives, and some even think that their children have died or have just abandoned them.

I noticed one morning that the fellow from Guinea was very depressed. I asked what was wrong and he said nothing, but I knew he was depressed since he had no definite knowledge about his case. He was worried about his future, and as a young man, he knew his life was wasting away. A bond was placed on him, and he didn't know how to raise the amount. His future was bleak because he didn't know when he would be deported even if he asked for voluntary deportation. I encouraged him and told him not to give up. I saw his eyes wet with tears, but he quickly dried them. I wondered, what would happen to him if his bond is not paid or deportation does not take place very soon. When will he get out? When is he going to be deported? But he was not the only one in this situation.

On the second day of my detention, I also noticed everyone going to their bunk beds late in the afternoon. The ones that didn't went to the bathroom, which was not much of a private place. Anyone in the dining room, which was a few feet from the beds could see who was in the bathroom. I was afraid of going in there. The first time I went there, I found it difficult to do number 1 and number 2 even though I needed to. But at 4:00 p.m., I discovered it was lockdown time. Lockdown is when every activity involving the detainees is brought to a standstill until they are counted and cleared. The lockdown period includes restricting every detainee to their beds until they are counted according to their photos. Every movement ceases, and only the officers are allowed to move around. During lockdown, the guard looks in your face to determine whether the face he is looking at matches the picture he has in his hand.

Before the day could end, someone invited me to a prayer meeting that took place at 8:00 p.m. At the prayer meeting, I met other detainees. One of the facilitators was a detainee from Angola. He was very young, maybe in his early twenties, but very passionate about God and the Bible. He must have had a true conversion experience before his arrest because he was more than a prison convert. There were also

Nigerians, Latinos, a fellow from Sri Lanka, and the Caribbean. But to my surprise, the preacher was the older gentleman from Nigeria I met during breakfast. He was ordained in the eighties and was serving a church in the United States. He had been in the United States for a long time. His wife and three kids were American citizens, but he was not. One would think because of the citizenship status of his wife, he would automatically gain his legality and walk out. In this case, it didn't seem that way. When I met him, he had been in detention for the past five months. He was previously in a county jail where he said he was mixed with hardened criminals and those convicted of a felony, an experience he characterized as one of the most degrading for him because he was not a criminal or charged with a felony. He had filed his case on several occasions and could only await his fate. But for now, he could only do what he knew best: preach the gospel of Jesus Christ and bring hope to those who came to listen. When I asked him what he missed most as a result of his detention, he responded, "My freedom."

Seated in the corner during the meeting was a very petite man. But his eyes and the eloquent articulation of his expressions showed a very educated man and someone who was also conversant with sophistication and culture. Yet there was the resonance of pain and agony hidden in the eloquence of his words. I decided to find the time to converse with him. The moment came, and it was one of those perplexing moments. He was a prominent Ghanaian journalist. He was at one time selected as one of two African journalists to attend a conference in the United States. He had written several articles and had worked with some prominent organizations in Ghana and the United States. At the time of his arrest, he was a student specializing in international politics. He was arrested on his way from Massachusetts to Alabama. When I met him, he had been in detention for six months. A bond was placed on him, and his personal belongings were taken away. He had depleted the funds he had, and without money, it was difficult to make contact with people on the outside. He was frustrated and had no money. As we spoke, I saw tears well up in his eyes, and I wanted to cry with him. God was his only source of refuge. By the end of my third day in detention, I had heard bits and pieces of stories about the length of time several of the detainees had spent in the facility. The maximum was about six years in this particular facility, not mentioning others around the country as they pondered their fate, as it were, in limbo.

The word *limbo* implies ambiguity. It is a Catholic doctrine which connotes a place situated between hell and heaven—a place of uncertainty for the dead, especially babies. The Catholic Church no longer holds to this doctrine because the logical necessity cannot be justified. The detainee to be deported is not certain of his fate since he awaits the decision of the judge, which may take a while in coming. Sometimes, because of the lack of breakthrough in his case, his uncertainty as to when he will be deported or his inability to pay the bond of $10,000, the detainee might ask to be voluntarily deported. But like many of the men I saw who have asked to be voluntarily deported, voluntary deportation does not get one out quickly. As a result, the detainee is frustrated and depressed. He does not know when he will be deported; he does not know whether he will be released, and since the bond is too high for his family to pay, he must painfully endure the ambiguity and uncertainty of his situation while wetting his pillow with tears in the middle of the night. With a $10,000 bond on his head, his fate is unpredictable. Furthermore, with no relative or friend of means around to shoulder the bond, the detainee is kept in limbo. He finds himself in this stalemate with his life wasting away. It is worst for the African who has no relative around. Unlike the Mexican who has the border to cross, the African has the Atlantic Ocean to cross and a fortune to pay in purchasing a ticket. As a result, his indefinite detention profits the prison industry.

A typical day in detention includes breakfast, lunch, and supper. Supper is either at 4:00 p.m. or 5:00 p.m. with breakfast the next day at five, six, or seven, depending on the specific detention facility. Because of the time lapse between supper and breakfast, one will automatically learn the tricks of not eating their entire ration but preserving some for the long night. The rest of the time is spent sleeping, conversing, or gazing obliviously into the surrounding walls that have come to define one's fate. In detention, I saw men, in whose eyes, one could see the loss of hope. In their eyes, hope had fled, and optimism—as an internal ingredient for perseverance—had evaporated. In the place of hope was desolation, and in the place of optimism was assimilation. The danger of assimilation is compromise and conformity, the tendency to accept one's condition of despair, anguish, pain, and humiliation as inevitable. Assimilation resists the catalytic nature of optimism, perseverance, and hopefulness. In their inherent nature of positive and transformative influences, optimism, perseverance, and hopefulness reject the subjugation and demoralizing conformity of assimilation. For assimilation in this context is the petulant acceptance of what has been decreed against your life, knowing that it seeks to destroy your hope, shatter your dreams, and kill your sense of ingenuity, dignity, and productivity.

But one afternoon I caught myself feeling comfortable with my blue uniform, strolling majestically in my brown detainee jacket and walking briskly in the black-and-white sneakers. I adopted the pattern of hiding and saving food in my brown jacket pockets for the night, of enjoying the meal of a detainee and subtly sliding into the identity of a detainee. Immediately, I caught myself. I said to myself; "don't be that comfortable; you cannot conform." I must transcend; otherwise this will be my end. I ran to the phone and called Dr. Fred Allen. "You have to get me out of here," I pleaded. I told him, "It is getting tense in here, and I must get out because I am losing me; self is evading me, and I am assuming a new identity." I called Rev. Larry Wimmer. I said, "you have to get me out of here." I called my district superintendent, Rev. Aida Fernandez. I told her to do all she could to get me out. She assured me she had spoken with the bishop Peter Weaver, and that they were working on my release. I told my self: "I will not accept this condition. I reject it, I resist it, and I refuse it. I will not die. I will live, I dare to live, and I must live." I began to pray and prayers I offered to God.

I prayed because this could not be my end. This end was a disruption of my existence. My detention was an interruption and an intrusion to my life. It was a disruption to my mission in life, an interruption of my meaning for living and an intrusion of my motive for existing and experiencing the exigencies of living for ideals beyond myself. "No, I cannot accept this" I said. If I have to call the entire world for my rescue, I will have to do it; but I cannot be comfortable in this blue uniform, this brown jacket, and these black-and-white sneakers, for they are signs of my death, my demise, and my destruction. To stop hoping, to stop believing in the impossible, in my innocence, and in the power of divine intervention is to cast my fate to the wind. I must not break down but must have "hope against hope."

On the fifth day in the morning, I was sitting in a secluded corner of the room when clean sheets and towels were supplied. I had not gotten used to the various announcements. I didn't get the supply of clean sheets. So I went to the officer on duty for some, but to my dismay, he said his boss had told him not to provide me with any clean sheets or towels. I said in my heart, "Lord, things are changing." I went to my bunk bed, it had no sheet on it, the green mattress in its harshness gazed at me in unforgiveness. I simply sat on it and refused to lie on it. I picked up my Bible and started to read. It was the only book I was allowed to take with me. I read the poetic books of Job, Ecclesiastes, Song of Songs, and was reading the book of Isaiah when this incident occurred. I turned to Isaiah 7 and found strength in verse 9: "If you do not stand firm in your faith, you will not stand at all." This occurred on the first of April.

There is danger in accepting your detention and incarceration as an act of fate and therefore become petulant about your surroundings and who you are. The danger is for one to stop pushing for release through legal means no matter how impossible it may seem. To relax and be petulant about the situation is to subject yourself to personal defeat. Especially if you believe in your innocence, there is no reason why you should accept the situation as your inevitable fate. I saw a young man around twenty-six to twenty-nine, laughing, joking, and annoying others as though walking in total freedom. He had a job in the kitchen for which he was proud and walked arrogantly. I heard he had been in there for a while, and it seemed he had accepted his condition as his destiny. For some, a moment of relaxation and ease is a moment of deep reflection and empowerment, a time to refill their quest and longing to be free. For others, it signals a moment of "settling down," of arriving at the point of escape from bills. In this context, the free food, false sense of security, the medical attention, the absence of bills to pay implies the acquisition of a level of stability.

At 3:00 p.m. on Tuesday, the first of April, my release was announced. The New England Annual Conference of the United Methodist Church had posted my bond, and I was told to pack whatever supplies were given to me in the pillowcase and proceed to the front desk in the hall to be processed, which I deliberately did. Standing at the desk in the hall, one of the fellows I met during breakfast came over to say good-bye. In the short time, we had become friends. He had been in detention for over five months and did not know what his fate was. A bond of $10, 000 was placed on him before I came, and he didn't know how in the world he was going to raise that amount. He asked the judge to deport him voluntarily but had not heard anything from the judge. I encouraged him to be strong and to keep on praying because God was able to do the impossible. So he came over to say good-bye. Standing there, I told him I was going to keep praying for him and that he shouldn't give up. Meanwhile, standing behind us was the officer on duty. He interrupted the conversation and said: "I will not release him." I turned around and jokingly asked, "Why?" The officer's response was shocking, and he was not joking. He said, "If I release him, I will not have a job." I was speechless. He saw the shock in my eyes, and I saw the rage in his eyes as his face turned red. Immediately another officer came to collect me to take me to the main desk for processing. That was a divine interruption. I knew he saw the shock on my face, and he knew I saw his wrath swelling in his face as it turned red, but I had escaped like a bird out of the snare of the fowler. I was whisked off, and in less than thirty minutes, I took off the brown jacket, the blue suit, and the black-and-white sneakers and returned the beddings. I was back on the outside in the world with the suddenness with which I entered into detention. I was tossed out just like I was tossed in. In five days, my entire life was transformed; my sense of consciousness informed; my perception about humanity, race, justice, and God reconfigured and influenced. I would no longer be the same. My eyes had been "opened." I had been allowed to witness humanity's inhumanity towards humanity, the incongruity of racial consciousness, the materialization of justice and the evidence of God's incomprehensible orchestration, and interruption of human activities. To my captor and to my warden I thought:

> In his eyes I am despised
> In his sight I am despaired
> In his eyes I should linger not
> In his sight I should languish
> Despised and appear not I must know
> Disappear and assert not I must acknowledge
> Who am I but a warning?
> Who am I but a warrant?
> A warning he knows not
> A warrant he sees not.
> Since in his eyes I am not (George Walters-Sleyon)

The conversation with the officer haunted me. Did he realize the implication of his statement? The young man that came to wish me good-bye was a classic example of thousands of people arrested and facing deportation but not knowing when they will be deported. In their frustration, like him, they have requested for voluntary deportation but still have not been deported. Some with the usual bond of $10,000 have languished in detention from months to years and still are not deported; only existing in limbo because of the ambiguity surrounding their detention.[14]

For the officer, because he must have a "job," detainees must be available. His daily bread depends upon the arrest and detention of illegal immigrants, unfortunately, in this case, lots of whom are of African descent. He is the reflection of the ethos of the prison industrial complex. The logic is that a certain number of detainees must be kept in the facility to maintain the momentum of detention and deportation in the public's eye. Since a certain number of detainees must be kept to maintain the detention facility operating, a certain number of arrests must be done to maintain the quota. In this case it seems justice and

---

[14.] The criminal basis of the detainees is unclear. According to the *Human Rights Watch 2007* report on the National Statistics on the Deportation for Crimes, there exists an ambiguity with respect to the reason for deportation. Only recently has the Immigration and Customs Enforcement (ICE) agency within the Department of Homeland Security provided statistics on criminal convictions warranting deportation from the United States. According to the *Human Rights Watch*, "For reasons that are unclear, in its regular press updates the agency always touts its deportation of violent criminals, but keeps vague the other categories of immigrants deported. The secrecy surrounding the criminal convictions forming the basis for deportation has been remarked upon by many attorneys, academics, and statistical researchers . . . In one press statement, announcing the deportation of 562 "criminals aliens,' ICE chose to highlight presumably three deportees who were removed for 'aggravated assault,' 'drug trafficking,' and 'lewd and lascivious acts on a child.'" It concludes by quoting a special observation from an immigration analysis unit from Syracuse University which declares, "Despite the interest in aggravated felonies, very little is currently known about how often aggravated felony provisions are in fact used. The government publishes no statistics on the number of individuals it has sought to deport, or actually deported, on aggravated felony grounds. A literature search has not turned up any other sources with relevant statistics." *www.hrw.org/reports/2007/us0707/6.htm*

security are not the fundamental impetus, but business, a certain amount of detainees must be kept and a certain amount released to balance the quota. The $10,000 reflects an adequate amount to have people lingering between actual deportation and indefinite detention. Someone might say, they should have known better not to have entered this country illegally or overstayed their visa. I met several gentlemen from Africa who have requested for voluntary deportation but have been there for more than six months. While in detention, their belongings were trashed, or did someone open them, take the valuables out, and is making some money out of the "trashed" bags and suitcases? They are guilty for entering the country as illegal, but the question is, how long will they linger between detention and indefinite deportation while their lives waste away as taxpayers' money bear the cost of their indefinite stay in limbo while supporting the operation of the commercial prison—industrial complex?

The effects of the prison-industrial complex and its social consequences are real. Its tools are the criminalization of the black man, the stereotyping of the black youth, the sequestering of the black adult male as an alibi to deviancy, racial differential in the sentencing process, three-strikes you are out, the war on drugs, high rate of racial profiling and its debilitating feeling. The consequences for the black youth growing up especially in the ghetto include social dislocation, a negative appreciation of self manifested in black-on-black crime and the weakening of the black family structure and the black community. These factors serve as impetus for the criminalization of the black man, high rate of recidivism, and the decline of eligible black men for marriage among others, thus reflecting the decline of the black family structure. The activities of the commercial prison—industrial complex reflect the fundamental means by which systemic racism plays itself out in the society. This project acknowledges the individual causes as relevant to the understanding of the situation but, to a large extent, interprets them within the larger historical, sociopolitical, and economic framework.

After reflecting on my situation, I have come to see both detention and deportation, especially for the black immigrant and domestic incarceration for the black man as influenced and informed not fundamentally by the crime committed. Instead, their detention and incarceration is fundamentally informed and influenced by their blackness, the racialization of their blackness and the criminalization of their blackness thus defining blackness as synonymous with crime. The alien of African origin, either directly from Africa or the Caribbean or other places in the Diaspora has a higher chance of being deported than any other race or nationality. In addition, the African American man has a higher chance of being arrested and incarcerated in America. The black immigrant man is criminalized just as much as the black man who is a citizen. Both are black men of African descent, subject to arbitrary arrest, racially profiled, racially sentenced, incarcerated or detained, and deported.

It is in this light that I want to theologically analyze the high rate of detention and incarceration of black men in America, its disproportionality, social consequences, and existential impact for the black man. I prefer to use "black men" or men of "African descent" instead of African, Caribbean, or African American. My experience and research has taught me that the differences are not as relevant as one might want to believe when looking at the prevailing statistics on the number of people detained for deportation and those incarcerated in county, state, and federal prisons and jails. The black man is known as a person of African descent or ancestry. While the use of people of African descent and black men or women may raise some questions for the white African, it should be clarified that the white African in America or Europe is not distinguished from the white American or European; they escape the experience of being African, and in that case, being a person of African descent in Europe and America denotes different meaning and interpretations for the black African or African American and the white African.

Footnote: On December 12th of 2008 my case was closed. Many thanks to my lawyers, and members of the New England Annual Conference of the United Methodist Church.

Chapter Two

The "Situation"

The underprivileged everywhere have long since abandoned any hope that this type of salvation deals with the crucial issues by which their days are turned into despair without consolation.
—Howard Thurman, *Jesus and the Disinherited*, Pg. 29-30

For the sake of one's children, in order to minimize the bill they must pay, one must be careful not to take refuge in any delusion-and the value placed on the color of the skin is always and forever a delusion.
—James Baldwin, *The Fire Next Time*, 1963

According to the *Pew Charitable Trust*, one in every one hundred persons in America is behind bars.[15] The Pew reports that "for some groups, the incarceration numbers are especially startling. While one

---

15. *www.pewcenteronthestates.org*: "*One in 100: Behind Bars in America 2008*," 5. "The United States incarcerates more than any country in the world, including the far more populous nation of China. At the start of the new year, the American penal system held more than 2.3 million adults. China was second, with 1.5 million people behind bars, and Russia was

in 30 men between the ages of 20 and 34 is behind bars, for black males in that age group the figure is one in nine."[16] White men age 18 or older is one in 106; Hispanic men age 18 or older is one in 36; black men ages 18 or older is one in 15; and black men especially ages 20-34 is one in 9.[17] Writing on the topic *Racial Impact Statements as a Means of Reducing Unwarranted Sentencing Disparities,* Marc Mauer of the Sentencing Project argues that:

> By the early 21st century, the scale of incarceration for African Americans had reached dramatic proportions. Projections by the Department of Justice show that if current trends continues, a black male born today has a one in three (32.2%) chance of spending time in state or federal prison in his lifetime. Comparable figures for Latino males are one in six (17.2%) and, for white males, one in seventeen (5.9%).[18]

Mauer goes on to state the causes for the rise in the detention and incarceration rate of black men. Among the many socioeconomic and legal factors, Mauer highlights the following factors as fundamental to the understanding of the increase in black imprisonment. They are: "Disproportionate crime rate, disparities in criminal justice processing, overlap of race and class effects" and finally "impact of 'race neutral' policies."[19]

This chapter presents an analysis of what I call "the situation." It looks at the statistical evidence and claims that justify the conclusion that the

---

a distant third with 890,000 inmates, according to the latest available figures. Beyond the sheer number of inmates, America also is the global leader in the rate at which it incarcerates its citizenry, outpacing nations like South Africa and Iran. In Germany, ninety-three people are in prison for every one hundred thousand adults and children. In the United States, the rate is roughly eight times that, or 750 per 100,000." 5.

[16]   Ibid.,3.: "*One in 100:Behind Bars in America 2008,*"

[17]   Ibid., 6, "*One in 100: Behind Bars in America 2008,*" 6.

[18]   Marc Mauer, *Racial Impact Statements as a Means of Reducing Unwarranted Sentencing Disparities,* rd_racialimpactstatements.pdf, 22, accessed 01/31/09.

[19]   Ibid., 23

LOCKED UP AND LOCKED DOWN

black man is disproportionally incarcerated in comparison to all other ethnic groups. My use of "situation" in quotation marks is intentional. The situation in this context is the problem that avails itself for theological and existential analysis. The situation also provides the necessity to interpret life as a detained and incarcerated Black man, its existential and social implications and the need for the Church to intervene.

According to Terry Tempest Williams in *The Covenant With Black America*, the necessity for us to take an introspective account of our activities in view of the sociopolitical and economic standing of black people in America today cannot be overstated. The urgency to assess our actions with respect to the future for the present generation and the need to transcend the trivialization of the present sociopolitical and economic condition of our community cannot be ignored. She writes, "The eyes of the future are looking back at us, and they are praying for us to see beyond our own time."[20] *The Covenant* does not mince words in presenting a descriptive analysis of the situation even though not the issues of black immigrants; it highlights the socioeconomic issues that affect every black person in America. Marian Wright Edelman in the *Statement of Purpose* in *The Covenant* tries to capture this dilemma by intimating that

> an unlevel playing field from birth contributes to many poor black children getting pulled into a cradle-to-prison-to-death pipeline that we must dismantle. Imprisonment is the new slavery for the black community. On average, states spend over three times as much per prisoner as per public school pupil.[21]

For James Bell, the process leading to incarceration for the black man is described as "cradle-to-prison superhighway"[22]: a "network of legislation, policy, practice, and structural racism that has fostered blacks being incarcerated at uncontrollable levels at increasingly younger ages for increasingly minor acts."[23] He believes

---

20.   *The Covenant With Black America* (Chicago, Third World Press, 2006), Introductory page.

21.   Ibid., xiii.

22.   Ibid., 49.

23.   Ibid., 49.

that the "warehousing" of black males as a rehabilitative measure has proven not to have achieved the intended result. On the contrary, incarceration has instead turned out to be a booming business. The impact of the cradle-to-prison superhighway is evident in the black family structure.[24] It was a crime in 1835 to teach a slave how to read. In 1991, two-thirds of those incarcerated were high school dropouts. In the absence of quality education and expectations, low teaching expectations and accountability, lack of resources and equipments for educational empowerment, the consequences are daunting.

For James Bell, "to reestablish integrity and fairness in the juvenile court system requires an emphasis on reducing racial disparities . . . we must use our collective voice to give voice to the voiceless"[25] he intimates. Bell sees the increased incarceration of black men and boys as a problem inherently established by the justice system, its historical perception and treatment of black men and boys. According to the *Human Rights Watch* 2001 report,

> the prison population of the United States is largely male: as is true around the world, men make up more than 90 percent of all prisoners. Also, in comparison with people outside prison, the inmate population is heavily weighted toward ethnic and racial minorities, particularly African Americans. Overall, African Americans make up some 44 percent of the prisoner population, while whites constitute 40 percent, Hispanics 15 percent, with other minorities making up the remaining 1 to 2 percent. Relative to their proportions in the U.S. population as a whole, black males are more than twice as likely to be incarcerated as Hispanic males and seven times as likely as whites.[26]

---

24. (Marc Mauer and Ryan Scott King, "*School and Prisons: 50 Years After Brown v. Board of Education,*" http: *www.sentencingproject.org/pdfs/brownboard.pdf,* the Sentencing Project.")

25. *The Covenant With Black America,* 51-52.

26. http://www.hrw.org/reports/2001/prison/report.html.

Echoing similar sentiments of dismay is Walter G. Muelder. Muelder is considered "one of the 20th century's greatest ethicists."[27] He was dean of Boston University School of Theology and served as professor of social ethics for twenty-seven years. Dr. Martin Luther King Jr. was one of his students. For Muelder, the sentencing process is referred to as "vengeful penology . . . aided and abetted by the recent growth of the commercial prison—industrial complex which has become a big $140 billion piece of the American economy."[28] As a Boston personalist who esteems the inherent dignity of all human beings, Muelder advanced the claim for the definition and execution of justice within the context of "persons-in-community.[29] Persons-in-community is Muelder's argument for a working solution that recognizes the "poor and disinherited" in the formulation of policies and the implementation of justice. It is in this light that Muelder expresses his frustration at the sentencing process and the high rate of incarceration and detention of minorities. He writes:

> What is the present situation in our prisons and jails? Three-fourths of our new inmates are African-Americans or Hispanics. Color-lining in arrests and sentencing is rampant. One-third of America's young African-American males are now in prison, on parole, or on probation. Furthermore, we are caught in the privatized prison-industrial complex. We have underdeveloped preventive institutions and after-care ministries. The two million persons in jail or prison are four times what it was 20 years ago . . . . There is no clear relationship of cause and effect except of a trend in the 'get tough' movement that advocates harsher sentences, mandatory minimum sentencing laws, bigger and fewer human prisons, minimal rehabilitation programs, decline in parole, militancy in the drug laws, the failing war on drugs,

---

27. J. Philip Wogaman (Ed), *Communitarian Ethics: Later Writings of Walter G. Muelder*, (Maine: The Preachers' Aid Society of New England in cooperation with BW press, 2007) xi.

28. Ibid., 20.

29. Ibid., 20.

three-strikes-and-you're-out laws. About 3,500 Americans (disproportionately African-American) sit on death row.[30]

For Muelder, as well as others who are equally disturbed about the sentencing process in the justice system, one possible option is reforming the sentencing process by adopting practices of restorative justice: "A restorative philosophy based on the ethical perspective that all people, including offenders and victims alike, are and should be treated as persons-in-commununity."[31] But while racial justice with respect to other civil rights concerns has historically been the most talked about issue for the Civil Rights Movement, contemporarily, Africans and people of African descent from the Caribbean are also increasingly being arrested, detained for deportation and are receiving little attention. According to Tamara kil Ja Kim Nopper,

> to put it simply, Black immigrants have higher numbers of deportations than Asian, Middle Eastern or White immigrants. For example, in 2002, there were 8, 921 total deportation of Black immigrants, whereas there were only 3, 090 total deportations for Whites and 4, 317 total deportations for Asians and Middle Easterners. Overall, this trend is consistent from 1993-2002.[32]

Unfortunately, the arrest and detention of black immigrants has not gotten the level of attention that other nationalities from Guatemala, El Salvador, Mexico, Honduras, etc., have received. Yet strangely enough, Nopper argues, "Black immigrants tend to have higher numbers of deportation than Asians and Whites, despite the fact that the rate of immigration from Africa and the Caribbean tend to be slower than the rate of Asian and Brown immigrants."[33]

---

[30]. Ibid., 20.

[31]. Ibid., 18.

[32]. *www.nathanielturner.com*: Tamara Kil Ja Kim Nopper; Black Immigrants are Deported in Higher Number than Asians and Middle Eastern Immigrants: Reconsidering Immigrants Rights' Challenge to 'Racial Justice' Work.

[33]. Ibid.,

Similarly, black immigrants had the highest rate of deportation for "criminal" activity than "non-criminal" activities between the period of 1993 and 2002.[34] As intimated, the distinction between what constitutes "criminal activities" and "non-criminal activities" warranting deportation is still ambiguous.[35] A high rate of criminal deportation is drug related. With the "war on drug," black communities around the country are seen as major targets. Unfortunately, as the above report suggests, immigrants of South Asia and the Middle East have gained more sympathy and received less deportation than people of African descent. In searching for the causes, one is immediately confronted with the association of black men with crime. This association is often done regardless of the absence of any criminal offence or record. Millions of Americans associate black men with crime and criminality. This thinking, that the black man is a criminal

---

[34.] Ibid., Tamara Kil Ja Kim Nopper:, "Given the limited attention given to Black immigrants in the immigrant rights discourse, there is of course little mention of the fact that between 1993 and 2002, Black immigrants tend to be deported more for criminal deportations than non-criminal deportations. Asians (including Middle Eastern and many "Muslim" nationalities), however, tended to be overwhelmingly deported for non-criminal deportations than criminal deportations. Between 1993 and 2002, the proportion of criminal deportations out of all Asian deportations ranged between 24-34%, reaching the peak of 34% in 1999. Compare that to the proportion of criminal deportations out of all Black deportations. During 1993 and 2002, criminal deportations of Black immigrants ranged between 57-75%, reaching the peak of 75% in 1996. In short, criminal deportations are more common for Black immigrants whereas the reverse is true for Asian immigrants."

[35.] Ibid., Tamara Kil Ja Kim Nopper., "Generally, criminal deportations mean that you were convicted of a crime, with the result that you are removed from the country after you serve your prison sentence. Any non-naturalized immigrant, regardless of status, can be forcibly removed from the US if they are convicted of an aggravated felony, which is any crime that carries a one-year or more sentence. Non-criminal deportations are usually deportations of immigrants who attempted to enter the US illegally or who overstayed their initial visa without adjusting their status."

before he can commit an offence, immediately highlights a historical problem in perception, assumption, and one that is paradigmatically problematic. Criminalizing the black man is done consciously and unconsciously because it is part of the social consciousness regarding black men in America. In reality, the black man is viewed suspiciously before his acceptance. This suspicion is often done regardless of his academic, professional, and economic attainment. The existential and psychological implication is enormous. It is in this context that one should seek to understand the black man behind bars, not as an African American or an African immigrant but as a black man struggling with his criminalization, his racialization, his socioeconomic condition, educational background and perhaps his crime.

The Imprisoned Black Men

The imprisoned black man in this context is the one behind bars. He might not have anyone to visit him, no one to bail him out or pay his bond. He is locked up. He screams and cries, but no one hears him. He is there because he is black, because he committed a crime, or he was caught with drugs for which he must pay with his life, or he is a victim and he knows it. On his own he must cry, and on his own he must fight against sexual coercion, intimidation, and threats from other men. If he was heterosexual, he might come out infected with HIV and infect others. As Christopher Marshall intimates in the biblical analysis, more men are raped in prison than women on the outside. In prisons they do not use condom. It is a generation at risk and a subtle destruction of the strength of the black community.

According to the *Human Rights Watch 2000-2001* report of three years of research, male prisoner-on-prisoner sexual abuse in the United State is very high for prisoners regardless of race or ethnicity. Rape takes place in prison every day. The anguish associated with this experience is enormous as evident in this account from the Human Rights Watch:

> A Florida prisoner whom we will identify only as P. R. was beaten, suffered a serious eye injury, and assaulted by an inmate armed with a knife, all due to his refusal to submit to anal sex. After six months of repeated threats and attacks by other inmates, at the end of his emotional endurance, he tried to commit suicide by slashing his wrists with a razor. In a letter to Human Rights Watch, he chronicled his unsuccessful

LOCKED UP AND LOCKED DOWN

efforts to induce prison authorities to protect him from abuse. Summing up these experiences, he wrote: "The opposite of compassion is not hatred, it's indifference."[36]

Once an inmate is abused, they "become trapped into a sexually subordinate role." Prisoners refer to the initial rape as "turning out." The victim is redefined as an object of sexual abuse. He has been proven to be weak, vulnerable, "female" in the eyes of other inmates. Regaining his "manhood" and the respect of other prisoners can be extremely difficult.[37] He is considered a "punk" or "turn out" and vulnerable to continuous sexual exploitation especially from the first perpetrator or perpetrators who often claim the role of protecting the victim from other inmates. The victim eventually becomes the property of the first perpetrator. According to the Human Rights Watch,

> victims of prison rape, in the most extreme cases, are literally the slaves of the perpetrators. Forced to satisfy another man's sexual appetites whenever he demands, they may also be responsible for washing his clothes, massaging his back, cooking his food, cleaning his cell, and myriad other chores. They are frequently "rented out" for sex, sold, or even auctioned off to other inmates, replicating the financial aspects of traditional slavery. Their most basic choices, like how to dress and whom to talk to, may be controlled by the person who "owns" them. Their name may be replaced by a female one. Like all forms of slavery, these situations are among the most degrading and dehumanizing experiences a person can undergo.[38]

The stigma of becoming the sexual property and slave of another inmate spreads from prison to prison. It becomes even more gruesome for the victim if he is sentenced to several years of imprisonment and detention since he will have to be transferred to other prisons and

---

[36] Human Rights Watch: http://www.hrw.org/reports/2001/prison/report. html

[37] Ibid.,

[38] Ibid.,

detention facilities. There are over 1.3million black men and boys exposed to this dilemma. Another report argues:

> According to the Federal Bureau of Prisons Report, approximately 9-20% of prison inmates are targets of aggressive sex acts during their incarceration. Several independent studies, however, place the percentage of homosexual rape significantly higher than this official calculation . . . Rape is one of the most serious safety issues in lockups, jails, and prison settings" (*http://beyond-the-illusion. com/files/issues/condom.txt*).

According to the Human Rights Watch, once a prisoner is sexually violated, they are marked for the period of time they are in prison.[39] It provides a perfect understanding for the HIV and AIDS epidemic in the black community since in most prison facilities, the use of condoms is not a policy neither encouraged. According to Maya Harris' writing in 2006,

> the mass incarceration of black people in America is a real and present danger. About one in every 265 white is incarcerated in local, states, or federal prison. By contrast, of the 36 million African Americans in this nation, almost one million of them are in prison; that is about one in every 36 black people who is behind bars somewhere in America. Blacks represent 44 percent of all incarcerated people in state and federal prison cells, yet account for only 13 percent of the American population.[40]

She asks the question that should concern all church leaders and policy makers: "How did we get here? And, given the current trend, can we change direction?"[41] Harris' question is a fundamental one and as such should be directed at the Church, not the Black church in particular but the entire Body of Christ: Blacks, Whites and Browns.

Her question calls for a lot of "looking within" or "soul searching." The high incarceration and detention rate of black men should not be

---

[39]   Ibid.,

[40]   *The Covenant with Black America,* 73.

[41]   *Ibid.,* 74.

strange to the Church in America.[42] Reform in the sentencing process can only take place when the Body of Christ stands up and says enough is enough.[43] According to Rodney L. Petersen, the influencing factors are race, racism, and its forms of racialization.

He argues that racism has permeated the facets of political and religious life as a result of its birth through the Church. For Petersen, the "issues of race" has "shaped civil politics and church polity . . . from the fifteenth century to the present . . . The destructive effects of racism in America are well documented from the quays of Charleston, to the auction blocks of Anacostia and the banks of Boston."[44] Petersen is a minister and director of the Boston Theological Institute. He also teaches at Boston University and is an advocate for restorative justice as an alternative to the Retributive system in the sentencing process. Petersen contends that in light of the increase in the prison population and the process of sentencing, there is a need for restorative justice. He writes, "In fact, one author (James Q. Whitman) has recently argued that our political system and the impact of slavery upon American society have helped to define the treatment meted out to those who have broken the law and are deemed criminals."[45] Petersen goes on to argue that racism and the privilege derived have informed the way America has defined people of African descent. For him,

---

[42] Kelly Brown Douglas, *What's Faith Got to Do with It?: Black Bodies /Christian Soul* (New York: Orbis Books, 2005).

[43] Gayraud S Wilmore,.*Black Religion and Black Radicalism: An Interpretation of the Religious History of Afro-American People* (New York: Orbis Books, 1994)

[44] Robert W. Pazmino, and Rodney L. Petersen, Eds. *Antioch Agenda,* (New Delhi: Indian Society for the Promotion of Christian Knowledge, 2007), 261, 263 He writes, "American culture has been shaped by the politics of race. We may not like this. We may try to deny this. We may not move beyond this even though the social and personal ills attributable to slavery have long been documented."

[45] Ibid., 264 (Whitman connects America's view of crime with the "leveling down" of our political system and with the impact of slavery upon American society such that the treatment meted out to criminals parallels that given to slavers.—See Whitman, James Q. *Criminals Punishment and the Widening Gap Between America and Europe* [New York: Oxford University Press, 2003]

racism, discriminatory behavior or prejudice towards those of another race, has been defined in terms of its ideological, structural and historic significance for the stratification of population in order to promote or maintain privilege. Race, along with socioeconomic status, ethnicity, gender, religion and other factors shapes how a person views the world.[46]

According to Petersen and Harris, there are salient factors serving as organizing principles for the perpetuation of this situation. They include historical racism in the justice system, the police's perception of black men, racial profiling, and the proclivity to suspect and arrest black men, the activities of the commercial prison—industrial complex and the criminalization of black men.[47] In addition, fundamental to the police's perception is the consciousness enforced by the media to the public of black men as "super-predator."[48] As a result, every black man is criminalized in the eyes of the public and viewed with skepticism

---

[46]   Ibid., 263.

[47]   U.S. Sentencing Commission, "*Special Report to Congress: Cocaine and Federal Sentencing Policy*" (February 1995)-http://www.ussc.gov/crack/execsum. pdf ("the 1991 Household Survey shows that 52 percent of those reporting crack use in the past year, as opposed to distribution, were white"); The Sentencing Project, "Crack Cocaine Sentencing Policy: Unjustified and Unreasonable, "available at *http://www.sentencingproject. org//pdfs/1003. pdf* (approximately 2/3 of crack users are white or Hispanic").

[48]   *The Covenant with Black America,* 67: In his book: *Body Count: Moral Poverty . . . And How to Win America's War Against Crime and Drugs* (New York: Simon& Schust, 1996) that Dilulio cowrote with William Bennett and John Walters, Dilulio suggests that "a late 1990s juvenile-crime explosion will be driven by a rising tide of . . . deeply troubled young men." He had earlier "attracted uncritical attention from the left and the right for his talk of the growth of a 'super-predator' caste of feral young males born of the absence civil society, families, and churches in many parts of America." Excerpted from "*The Real John Dilulio*" by Eli Lehrer of The Heritage Foundation, February 7, 2001, archived at *http://www.heritage.org.*

and suspicion regardless of who he is or where he comes from. The criminalization of the black man therefore creates a prism through which the black man and youth are viewed, no matter how wrong and limited that prism is. It is enforced by the thinking that blacks commit more crime than whites, Hispanic, or any other nationality and therefore must be treated as such. In that case, the thinking that black men commit more crime is legitimized by the media and justified by judicial means, thus formulating a cultural consciousness and imagination. For W. E. B. Du Bois,

> Negroes came to look upon courts as instruments of injustice and oppression, and upon those convicted in them as martyrs and victims . . . I have seen twelve-year-old boys working in chains on the public streets of Atlanta, directly in front of the schools, in company with old and hardened criminals; and this indiscriminate mingling of men and women and children makes the chain-gangs perfect schools of crime and debauchery. (Du Bois, *Souls of Black Folk pg. 108*)

Incarceration and detention are not places for reform, restoration, and transformation, but in most cases, places where new tricks are learned and criminal behaviors are reinforced through the mingling of hardened and young criminals.

The Why Factor

> *O earth, do not cover my blood; may my cry never be laid to rest!*
> *Even now my witness is in heaven; my advocate is on high. My*
> *intercessor is my friend as my eyes pour out tears to God; on behalf*
> *of a man he pleads with God as a man pleads for his friend.*
> —Job 16:18-21

According to the Bureau of Justice 2005 statistic report, racial discrimination in the criminal justice system adversely influenced the sentencing process. It reports that there were 3,145 black male inmates per 100,000 in comparison to 471 white male inmates per 100,000. The Sentencing Project in its July 2007 analysis of racial disparity in prison sentencing report revealed wide variation in incarceration by state, with states Northeast and Midwest exhibiting the greatest black-to-white disparity in incarceration. In five states-Iowa, Vermont, New Jersey, Connecticut, and Wisconsin-black men are incarcerated at (a rate) more than ten times than whites.[49]

The study makes the prediction that if there is no change in this trend we should expect "one in three black males and one in six Hispanic males" going to prison, confirming the predictions of the *Pew Charitable Trust* as quoted earlier.[50] Ashley Nellis and her colleagues in their article: *Criminal Justice: Race and Criminal Justice* bemoans the dire effects of race in the sentencing process and the social consequences. They argue that:

> Over 30 years of 'get tough' solutions to crime in the United States have produced the world's largest prison population and incarceration rate, over 60% of whom are people of color. A large proportion of today's prisoners are victims of the failed 'War on Drugs,' which pulled in thousands of people convicted of low-level offenses for long, mandatory sentences."[51]

The high rate of incarceration and detention is overwhelmingly seen as influenced by the following factors:

The war on drugs. The most common offense that blacks are imprisoned for is drug offences.[52] This war employs racially based measures to prosecute blacks. Drugs in the black community is

---

[49]. *http://www.sentencingproject.org/NewsDetails.aspx?NewsID=454*

[50]. Ibid.,

[51]. *Criminal Justice: Race and Criminal* in *Compact for Racial Justice: An Agenda for Fairness and United* (A proactive plan for fairness and unity in our communities, politics, the economy and the law, Applied Research Center) rd_compact_final.pdf, 17 (Accessed: 01/31/09).

[52]. *http://www.sentencingproject.org/NewsDetails.*aspx?NewsID=454 9: rd_crisisoftheyoung[1].pdf "While the numbers of inmates in the federal prison system are smaller overall, the scale of the increase has been similar. The 4,900 federal drug offenders in 1980 represented 25% of the inmate population. This grew to 51,700, or 60%, by 1995.

considered a crime or a black individual caught with drugs is considered a criminal. Drugs in the white community is considered a medical problem or a white person caught with drugs is not considered a criminal but a health problem. The white person is sent to a rehabilitation center. The black individual is criminalized and incarcerated. According to the Sentencing Project,

> The prosecution of the drug war has disproportionately affected communities of color. Surveys conducted by the Department of Health and Human Services estimate that blacks constitute 13.3% of monthly drug users, yet blacks represent 32.5% of persons arrested for drug offenses. Of all persons imprisoned for drug offenses, three fourths are blacks or Latino. These disparities result in large part through a two-tiered application of the drug war. In communities with substantial resources, drug abuse is primarily addressed as a public health problem utilizing prevention and treatment approaches. In low-income communities those resources are in short supply and drug problems are more likely to be addressed through the criminal justice system.[53]

In addition, blacks caught with drugs are more harshly penalized than any other group in the country. The most disturbing penalty

---

Looking at prisons and jails combined, there are now an estimated 400, 000 inmates either awaiting trail or serving time for a drug offense, out of a total inmate population of 1.7million. As these policies are implemented, they have increasingly affected African American and Hispanic communities. The African American proportion of drug arrests has risen from 25% in 1980 to 37% in 1995. Hispanic and African American inmates are more likely than non-Hispanic whites to be incarcerated for a drug offense. As of 1991, 33% of Hispanic state prison inmates had been convicted of a drug offense, 25% of blacks, 12% of non-Hispanic whites."

[53.] www.Sentencingproject.org/rd_brownvboard[1].pdf (Substances Abuse and Mental Health Service Administration, Office of Applied Studies, National Survey on Drug Use and Health, 2002. Table 1. 26A) 3.

meted out in most drug related cases disproportionably affecting black youths is the three-strike-you-are-out rule.

Three-strikes-and-you-are-out is the policy that two prior arrests making up the third will earn you a twenty-five year or life imprisonment. The implementation of this measure implies that a prior offense record jeopardizes an individual's chance of getting off. Most black men will, as the studies have shown, have a prior conviction record; therefore, black men who are convicted will probably experience more three-strike penalties than any other racial group. The Sentencing Project predicts that

> policies that impose harsher penalties based on criminal history will have a disproportionate effect on African Americans. In California, for example, blacks constitute 29% of the population, but 44.7% of the persons serving a "three strikes" sentence (California Department of Corrections. Second and Third Strikers in the Institution Population. Sacramento, CA: Data Analysis Unit. (February 2004). These disparities take on added significance due to the extreme disparities created by such policies. A non-violent offense in California that might otherwise lead to no more than a few years in prison becomes a sentence of 25 years to life when treated as a third strike offense.[54]

Pat Nolan was a Republican legislator who had a long political career and was well connected. His résumé shows he went to law school at USC Law School. But in the 1990s, Nolan was convicted and imprisoned. Before his imprisonment, Nolan was an avid advocate for harsher prison measures and sentencing. Unfortunately, he was caught receiving checks from an undercover agent of the FBI and sentenced to twenty-six months. While in prison, he got converted, and upon his release, he became a champion for reformed and better treatment for prisoners in the criminal justice system. Nolan experienced a reality check together with his conversion experience; it was about the sober reality of depersonalization, hopelessness, together with the shock a prisoner encounters when released

---

[54.] *www.Sentencingproject.org/rd_brownvboard[1].pdf 4,*

LOCKED UP AND LOCKED DOWN

without the requisite skills to survive. He describes his experience as follows:

> You're an amputee, cut off from family, community, job, church, and, with your stump still bleeding, you're tossed into this boiling cauldron of anger, hatred, bitterness, sexual repression, and you're totally disrespected—screamed at—by officers all the times . . . You are sneered at with venom and told repeatedly, "You ain't got nothing coming."
>
> The implication is that you are nothing, you've come from nothing and you will be nothing. You are worthless. You have no future. None . . . . As a legislator, I had assumed that our prisons were not only preparing people for success upon release, but also helping these damaged men develop a moral compass, and ensuring that they analyzed the bad decisions that got them in trouble, I was wrong.[55]

Since coming out, Nolan has committed his life to prison reform. According to Human Rights Watch, the incarceration rate increased between 1979 and 1990, while blacks' incarceration rate in state and federal jails increased from 39 to 53%. Nationally, blacks are incarcerated at a rate of 8.2, twice the rate of whites. One in every twenty black men over the age of eighteen is in state or federal prison.[56]

---

[55] *http://www.latimes.com/news/local/la-me-nolan5jul05*,1, 2867656,f

[56] *http://www.hrw.org/reports/2000/usa/Rcedrg00-01.htm* sees this document for detail: "The disproportionate representation of black Americans in the U.S. criminal justice system is well documented. Blacks comprise 13 percent of the national population, but 30 percent of people arrested, 41 percent of people in jail, and 49 percent of those in prison. Nine percent of all black adults are under some form of correctional supervision (in jail or prison, on probation or parole), compared to two percent of white adults. One in three black men between the ages of 20 and 29 was either in jail or prison, or on parole or probation in 1995. one in ten black men in their twenties and early thirties is in prison or jail. Thirteen percent of the black adult male population has lost the right to vote because of felony disenfranchisement laws."

With the latest report, blacks make up 12-13% of the population of the United States but account for 51% of the prison population.

Contributing in several ways to the high rate of detention and incarceration[57] is the thinking that blacks are more violent and, therefore, a cause for their containment. This assumption according to most legal analysts is a misnomer. Police bias and prejudice have contributed to the disproportion in the incarceration rate of black men.[58] Black youths are treated differently than white youths with similar records in the juvenile justice system.[59] In 2001, it was discovered that only 13% of blacks were known to have used drugs

---

[57] p. 37; Parenti, p. 11 www. sentencingproject.org/women_cjs_ overview(1)[1].pdf

[58] www. sentencingproject.org/women_cjs_over view(1)[1].pdf "Hindelang (1978) attempted to assess the extent to which black overrepresentation in arrest statistics reflects differential involvement by blacks in crime or differential selection of blacks for arrest by the police. He compared FBI arrest statistics for common-law, personal crimes with the racial identifi cation of offenders made by victims of the National Victimization Panel. While finding some evidence of police bias, he concluded that the data for rape, robbery and assault are generally consistent with official data on arrests and support the differential involvement hypothesis. As further evidence in support of the differential involvement hypothesis for black overrepresentation in arrest statistics, Silverman (1978) reported that Puerto Rican New Yorkers, who are, as a group, poorer and less educated than black New Yorkers, have only one-third the arrest rate of blacks for violent crimes. Mexican Americans in south Texas have one-eighth the conviction rate of black Texans for robbery."

[59] Ibid., "According to the Justice Department's study, among white youths offenders, 66% are referred to juvenile courts, while only 31% of the African American youth are taken there. Blacks comprise 44% of those detained in juvenile jail, 46% of all those tried in adult criminal courts, as well as 58% of all juveniles who are warehoused in adult prison. This means that for young African Americans who are arrested and charged with a crime, they are six times more likely to be assigned to prisons than white youth offenders."

but disproportionately incarcerated for drug offenses than any other minority group.[60] Most crack cocaine users are white but blacks are more easily and harshly sentenced than whites for drug offenses.[61] According to Marc Mauer, director of the Sentencing Project, between the 1970s and 2007, the incarceration rate increased at 500% with approximately 2.2 million individuals imprisoned across the country.[62] Blacks make up more than one million of this amount.[63] In presenting the national picture on "substantial racial disparity" Mauer writes that

> the American prison and jail system is defined by an entrenched racial disparity in the population of incarcerated people. The national incarceration rate for whites is 412 per 100,000 residents, compared to 2, 290 for African Americans, and 742 for Hispanics. These figures mean that 2.3% of all African Americans are incarcerated, compared to 0.4% of

---

60.   Ibid. "In the first five years after the passage of the Omnibus Anti-Drug Act of 1986, African Americans accounted for more than 80 percent of the increase in incarcerated drug offenders. In state facilities during that period, the rate of black citizens incarcerated increased by 465. 5 percent, compared to a 110.6 percent increase for whites. One may guess that this disparity is due to extremely high drug use by blacks, but according to the US Sentencing Commission, only 13 percent of all drug users are blacks which matches their percent in the population."

61.   www. sentencingproject.org/women_cjs_overview(1)[1]. "A 1992 study showed that no white defendants had been prosecuted federally on crack charges in 17 states and many cities. Only one white person had been convicted in federal courts in California, two in Texas, three in New York and two in Pennsylvania. This is in spite of the fact that many people believe that most crack cocaine users are black but according to federal surveys, most crack cocaine users are white (a 1995 report put the figure at 52 percent)."

62.   The Sentencing Project: "Uneven Justice: State Rates of Incarceration by Race and Ethnicity," Marc Mauer and Ryan S. King, July 2007 (rd_stateratesofi ncbyraceandethnicity[1].pdf.

63.   Ibid 5(rd_stateratesofi ncbyraceandethnicity[1].pdf.

whites and 0.7% of Hispanics." Furthermore, "while these overall rates of incarceration are all at record highs, they fail to reflect the concentrated impact of incarceration among young African American males in particular, many of whom reside in disadvantaged neighborhoods. One in nine (11.7%) African-American males between the ages of 25 and 29 are currently incarcerated in a prison or jail.[64]

As Mauer mentioned, the link between poverty and crime, dysfunctional family structures, poor quality education, and illiteracy continue to be highlighted as major contributing factors. Black men are the most to be caught in poverty. They make up the highest amount of the incarcerated and juvenile population in detention in the Department of Youth Services or DYS. Incarceration has come to be viewed as a common occurrence for most black men and the black community.[65] Black youths make up the highest amount of those put into Special Education Programs, a recipe for stagnation, digression and destruction in the educational development of a child. States with large white population and small black population tend to have the highest rate of black incarceration and detention.[66] Other causes include emphasis on punitive measures rather than rehabilitation, the

---

[64.]   Ibid 4 (rd_stateratesofi ncbyraceandethnicity[1].pdf

[65.]   *American Sociological Review*, 2004, Vol. 69 (April: 151-169), Mass_ Imprisonment_and_the_life_Race_and_Class_Ineq[1].pdf p 151 "High incarceration rates led researchers to claim that prison time had become a normal part of the early adulthood for black men in poor urban neighborhoods."

[66.]   *American Sociological Review*, 2004, Vol. 69 (April: 151-169), 153 "Strongest evidence for racially differential treatment is found for some offenses and in some jurisdictions rather than at the aggregate level. African Americans are at especially high risk of incarceration, given their arrest rates, for drugs crimes and burglary. States with large white populations also tend to incarcerate blacks at a high rate, controlling for race-specific arrest rates and demographic variables. A large residual racial disparity in imprisonment thus appears due to the differential treatment of African Americans by police and the courts."

so-called higher crime rate in the black community,[67] "concentrated" poverty which includes lack of access to quality education, lack of access to transition to "adult roles-employment, college education, and stable relationships,"[68] low-income, lack of education and career skills, and single parenting. Concentrated poverty is a degree of poverty that reflects an intrinsic "socioeconomic disadvantage."[69]It is characterized by dilapidated city environment, high rate of poverty, homelessness, joblessness, infant mortality rate, and poor housing environment. The number of blacks living in ghetto areas has increased to 38 percent.[70] Unemployment prior to arrest is also a large factor.

As previously intimated, the criminalization of the black man in America continues to be a major factor. Criminalization engenders arbitrary arrest and harsher punitive measures. Criminalization as an impetus maintains the crime statistics because it presents the black man as a criminal. In maintaining the statistics by whatever means possible, the black person's sense of personhood is disregarded and distorted in the eyes of every citizen and visitor who comes to the United States. In perpetuating the stereotype that black men are criminals and

---

67. *www.Sentencingproject.org/rd_brownvboard[1].pdf*, p. 2 "Crime Rate: Higher rates of involvement in some crimes explain part of the high rate of black imprisonment. For property offenses, blacks constituted 29% of arrests in 2002 and for violent offenses, 38%; these compared to the 12.3 % black proportion of the total population. (Note that an arrest may not always be an accurate indicator of involvement in crime, but it often remains the best means of approximating this measure.) However, criminologist Alfred Blumstein, in a study on race and imprisonment, noted that higher arrest rates for drugs crimes in particular were not correlated with higher rates of use in the general population. In short, drug arrest patterns were not a reliable indicator of drug offending, because African-Americans are arrested more frequently than their rate of drug use would suggest" (Blumstein, Alfred. (1993). "Racial Disproportionality of U.S. Prison Population Revisited," University of Colorado Law Review, Vol. 64, 743-760).

68. Ibid., 2

69. Ibid., 3

70. Ibid., 3-5

therefore must be detained and incarcerated, a suspicious notion of the black man is created, subjecting him to arbitrary arrest. In view of the disproportionality in black immigrants arrest and detention, criminalization and racism provides little distinction between African Americans and African immigrants. The primary targets are black men. The criminalization of the black man eventually makes it difficult for most black men to move up economically without their subjection to racial scrutiny. If they possess criminal records, they are doomed for a long time and become economically marginalized. One thing is evident, their doom and disempowerment are often the result of their criminalization, their arbitrary arrest, and their sentencing, their detention, incarceration and the racialization of their crime rather than the crime itself.[71]

> **The movement of the Spirit of God in the hearts of men often calls them to act against the spirit of their times or causes them to anticipate a spirit which is yet in the making. In a moment of dedication, they are given wisdom and courage to dare a deed that challenges and to kindle a hope that inspires (Howard Thurman:** *Footprints of a Dream***).**

Social Consequences

The large-scale imprisonment of black men also has its social repercussions. For the black man, it reflects his disempowerment. Embedded within this sociological effect is a grave economic disempowerment and dependency. This kind of dependency eventually engenders a generational impact that perpetuates generational poverty. For in their old age when they are released, many of them must now depend upon the welfare system for survival. Economic dependency leads to economic marginalization and ultimate isolation. The marginalized eventually feels deranged. In many cases, they must take their own lives because of a deep sense of frustration or do

---

[71.] Jennifer C. Karberg, and Beck, Allen J. *"Trends in U.S. Correctional Populations: Findings from the Bureau of Justice Statistics."* Presented at the National Committee on Community Corrections Meeting, Washington, DC, April 16, 2004.

LOCKED UP AND LOCKED DOWN

something to return to prison, thus accounting for the high recidivism rate among black men and youths.

This cycle of confinement reflects the dilemma of the young black man. Imprisoned in his teens, he must stay in jail, imprisonment, or detention until he is an adult. Unfortunately, if he did not complete high school before his arrest, he is at a great disadvantage upon his release. He lacks the social and employment skills necessary to support himself in the society. Furthermore, society expects him to be a good citizen, but according to Hegel's view on crime and punishment, he is rightless. If we examine Hegel's assertion once again, we realize that in its literal interpretation, the black man with a criminal record will always be considered a criminal in the world. As a result of his criminal act, he has lost his right to be a viable participator and contributor in the society. His crime nullifies both his inherent right and his concrete right as a citizen since the crime committed incurs an "infinite injury" against both his concrete and abstract rights. But as a black man, he was a suspect even before his crime. According to Hegel, when he commits a crime, he must pay the due penalty for his crime, but after paying the due penalty for his crime, he must remain a criminal for life even if his punishment was pardoned. The fact that he has committed a crime means he must remain a criminal. But what if he was criminalized before his crime, and even after paying the due penalty for his crime, why should he be considered an inherent criminal?[72] For the black man, his criminalization precedes him. He is criminalized before committing a crime, and when he commits a crime, his crime induces harsher punishment because his crime is associated with his racial identity. Like himself, his crime is racialized. He cannot get a job even if he is employable, he cannot easily buy a home, he cannot receive federal aid if he wants to go to school, he cannot work for the government, and he cannot participate in the political process of his country because his crime and not his punishment disqualifies him from voting.[73] He has already served the due punishment for his crime and served his time, but he is still a criminal. In 2001, 13% of all black men could not vote because of conviction records. That number is approximately 1.4 million. The 51% of those locked up in 2001 were

---

72. Hegel, PR. 282.

73. *http://www.sentencingproject.org/issueAreaHome.aspx?IssueID=4.*

black men according to the 1998 Criminal Justice Statistics. He has paid for his crime in prison, yet he is still a criminal and a criminal for life; a black criminal not just a criminal. His is a classic case for economic marginalization and generational impoverishment. There are many in this situation and most of them are black men.

The social consequences are felt on different levels.[74] The impact of over a million black men in jail raises the questions of dysfunctional families, fatherlessness, and black boys growing up without role models in the homes.[75] According to Mauer the "ripple effect" of the increase in the incarceration of black men has systematically affected the black family structure. He argues that:

> The rate of incarceration for African Americans in the United States is now at a level that is seriously affecting life prospect for the generation of black children growing up today. In addition, the ripple effects of current policy now extend the impact of incarceration beyond just the individual in prison, but to families and communities as well.[76]

It provides a perfect opportunity that gangs have seen fit to capitalize upon by providing "protection," "financial security," a "sense of belonging," and "self-confidence" as the black prison and detention population increases every day.[77] While black men have the highest rate of incarceration, there is a growing number of black women going

---

74. *www.Sentencingproject.org/rd_brownvboard[1].pdf.* 5

75. Ibid., 5 "One of every 14 black children has a parent in prison on any given day; over the course of childhood, the figures would be much higher. Family formation, particularly in urban areas heavily affected by incarceration, is also affected by these trends. In the highest incarceration neighborhoods of Washington, D.C., the absence of black men has created a gender ratio of only 62 men for every 100 women."

76. Marc Mauer, rd_racialimpactstatements.pdf, 46, (Accessed 01/31/09

77. Ibid., 12, 1999. rd_crisisoftheyoung[1].pdf "It is likely that the prison population overall will continue to grow in coming years. A survey of state correction agencies found that state officials projected that the 1994 prison population would rise by 51% by the year 2000. Despite falling crime rates, a variety of sentencing policies adopted in the past

LOCKED UP AND LOCKED DOWN 65

into detention. A little of over 30 % of black women are incarcerated. According to the Sentencing Project,

> the likelihood that children will have parents who are incarcerated is disproportionately linked to race. In 1990, one of every 14 black children had a parent in prison, compared with one in every 125 white children. Black children are almost (more) likely than white children to have a parent in prison and Hispanic children are 3 times more likely.[78]

Thus we are beginning to witness the disintegration of the black family structure in our contemporary time as a result of incarceration and detention. According to Pope John Paul II, the family is the most important means for the propagation of the society and the church. The family is seen as the child's first introduction to life and love as "stabilizing influences" for the society and the Church. He writes,

> It is the first and irreplaceable school of life, an example and stimulus for the broader community relationship marked by respect, justice dialogue and love . . . . The family is thus . . . the place of origin and the most effective means for humanizing and personalizing society: it makes an original contribution in depth to building up the world, by making possible a life that is possibly speaking human, in particular by guarding and transmitting virtues and "values."[79]

---

fifteen years are contributing to the burgeoning of the prison population. These include the mandatory sentencing laws now in effect in all fifty states and the federal system, the 'three-strikes-and-you're-out' law in nearly half the states, and newly-adopted 'truth sentencing' policies that will increase the time served in prison for many offenders by requiring that they serve 85% of their sentence. Preliminary indications of this trend are already evident in research by the Bureau of Justice Statistics, which show that the percentage served prior to release increased from 38% in 1990 to 44% in 1996."

78. www. sentencingproject.org/women_cjs_overview(1)[1].pdf.

79. *Familiaris Consortio*, 43

For the black man detained for deportation, he is confronted with the tragedy of separation from his family. Often, the men are deported leaving their wives behind with one or two children or even more. This leaves the mothers working two or three jobs while taking care of the children. Take for instance the case of Georgina and Howard Facey.

Georgina, an African American, and Howard, a Jamaican, got married in 1997 and gave birth to four children who are American citizens. Georgina filed immigration papers for her husband immediately. Unfortunately, it took six years before they heard anything about the case. At the advice of a lawyer, Howard went to the immigration office at Federal Plaza in New York to inquire about his papers but was arrested upon his inquiry. He was detained and processed for deportation to Jamaica. Howard was not given the opportunity to see a judge. According to Georgina,

> Howard called home from JFK airport at 6:00 a.m. to say that he was being deported. My heart sank, but I did not have the time to break down. I had to get our three kids ready for school and rush to work at a local drugstore. Letisha, Kristina, and Christopher ask for their dad every day. Their grades are dropping, and the school counselor says they are depressed. Childcare is really hard. When a family friend who was supposed to get Christopher from school was late a few times, the principal threatened to call Children's Services. With all this pressure, I don't have the time to properly treat my heart condition . . . Back . . . in the Caribbean, no one will hire a U.S. deportee.[80]

In a statement, Howard narrates his ordeal:

> I went to Federal Plaza to pick up my work forms. When I went before "a few months ago" they told me to just come back and things would be ready. The forms were ready, but the officers would not give them to me. They told me I had some error years ago. I did not really know what they were talking about. But they shackled my hands and feet, and put

---

80. *www.familiesoffreedom.org* April 2, 2008 at 8:00 p.m.

a chain around my waist. Then they sent me over to a jail for a few days, and then to the airport. I felt so awful. I couldn't believe it . . . . I long to be with my girls.[81]

During the ordeal, Georgina did not give up. She writes, "On Wednesday we are going to our Congressman Ed Towns to ask for help. We are also going to our Senators. We vote them into office to protect our families. Hopefully our Congressman and Senators can help reunite my family soon."[82] This was 2004. Hopefully, Howard may have joined his family back in the United States or not. This story was taken from the *Families of Freedom* Web site.

Imprisonment Is Not a Rite of Passage

> *Who can discern his errors forgive my hidden faults. Keep your servant also from willful sins; may they not rule over me. Then will I be blameless, innocent of great transgression. May the words of my mouth and the meditation of my heart be pleasing in your sight, O Lord, my Rock and my Redeemer.*
> —Psalm 19: 12-14

A culture of arrest, detention, and incarceration for any group of people eventually transforms itself into a culture of life. This is because the experience becomes a shared experience in the community. In this context, instead of the black child experiencing a normal and steady introduction to society and societal values, raised with the consciousness of participating in society, he is raised on the experience and consciousness of a subculture that negates a proper social development. The consequences are profound because he might think incarceration connotes manliness and dominance. As a result, his paradigm for life and success is skewed, and his sense of progress distorted. His ability to properly behave in society and by societal norms is impaired. His life is transformed by the shared experience of imprisonment and incarceration. The black child that grows up in this environment perceives incarceration as a badge of honor especially

---

81. Ibid.,

82. Ibid.,

when his father and brothers have been incarcerated before. The assumption is that one has done something to deserve the society and the world's attention; in essence, he has gained a form of recognition and has "graduated" into "manhood." For the Sentencing Projects, detention and incarceration have become aspects of the maturing process for most black men.

> The approaches taken (imprisonment and racially formulated forms of policies implementations) to address this problem over the past several decades have created a situation whereby imprisonment has come to be seen as an almost inevitable aspect of the maturing process for black men, and increasingly for black women.[83]

While individual and family responsibilities largely ought to minimize the negative perception of the society on the growth of the child, we see that the very family structure has been greatly influenced by the social consciousness of negativity, especially manifested in the life of the urban black youth. According to available data, "A black male born in 1991 has a 29% chance of spending time in prison at some point in his life. The figure for white males is 4%, and for Hispanics, 16%."[84] Blacks easily acquire criminal records because they are black since the sociohistorical consciousness of the society informs and enforced the consciousness that black men especially are criminals. According to Mark Mauer of the Sentencing Project, "Offenses by blacks are more likely to lead to arrest than those of whites. While the self-reported involvement of adolescent males represents a 3:2 black/white deferential, the arrest ratio is 4:1."[85]

Why should incarceration be viewed as a rite of passage? It is due to the fact that the black youth is stereotyped before he can define his own reality. This becomes even more pronounced if he grows up in the ghetto and in a dysfunctional family structure. He might grow up with

---

83. *www.Sentencingproject.org/rd_brownvboard[1].pdf* 5.

84. Mauer, Marc, *The Crisis of the Young African American Male and the Criminal Justice System*, (D.C, prepared for the U.S. Commission on Civil Rights, April 15-16, 1999), rd_crisisoftheyoung[1].pdf p. 3

85. Ibid., 3.

the constant feeling of being estranged from society. He is conscious of the feeling of being an outsider because of his race and skin color, even though an "insider." Without the opportunity for normal social development into adulthood, the slightest misbehavior is viewed as deviancy or intellectual deficiency. He is sent to DYS or placed in special education category and there he finds it difficult to progress onto college. Black youths make up the highest amount of students sent to special education programs. But this is the beginning of his demise and the shattering of his evolving world. As a black youth who commits crime, a judge may not look kindly on him to understand where he is coming from but quickly sentence him to an adult prison where an even more distorted process of mental and psychological development must take place: in the midst of hardened criminals. His life is on the verge of destruction and his potential and zest for life twisted as he leaves the prison walls with a distorted self-image and worldview.

Upon his release from prison, he is confronted with an economic dilemma. He might not have completed high school and might not have learned any trade or vocation behind bars. He comes out uneducated, unskilled, and untrained and is lost in the world. His only option is to depend upon his natural strength, which renders him susceptible to violence, crime, abuse, and self-destruction. If he is not assisted, his chances for success in life continue to narrow, and as a result, imprisonment no longer becomes a choice but the only option to avoid his woes.

Not only is he confronted with an economic dilemma, he is also confronted with a political dilemma. His right as a citizen was eclipsed from him before he came to the consciousness of it. When he came to understand that he had rights, they were already taken away. His innocence and naivety were not pardoned. He must now live rightless as a citizen. He ends up being a liability, but he must still pay his dues to society, yet he cannot work and he cannot survive independently. He is rightless and finds it difficult to be responsible to a wife, a child, and a family. He cannot work to provide for his family because he served some time in jail for a crime he committed or did not commit. He served the time but must be stigmatized and isolated especially as a black man. He is disempowered as a man and rightless. Now he must forever abide by the rules of other men who like him are citizens but, unlike him, have rights. This is the dilemma of the incarcerated black man and black youth.

He must tell himself like the Psalmist, "I shall not die but live," though "the waves of death swirled about me and the torrents of destruction overwhelm me," I shall not die but live. "Some trust in chariots and some trust in horses but I will trust in the Lord." I shall not die but live. "God is my refuge and strength, an ever-present help in time of trouble." I shall not die but live. His only source of hope is the "spark of the divine" within, one that stubbornly pulls us toward the source of our being. But how will he come to the understanding of this strength within if the Church does not see the need to intervene? There are multitude of men who are caught in this anxiety, this anarchy, and bewilderment within. Some have nowhere to go and no one to run to; they must return to imprisonment. How painful this must be.[86]

A problematic assumption that also informs our sociopolitical and economic consciousness is the constant attempt to equate crime and criminality with poverty: That the poor person is a criminal and that poverty implies moral and ethical incontinence. In this case, the poor person is susceptible to every form of suspicion.[87] The belief is that people are poor because they are immoral and lazy. Rich people are moral and ethical and should be catered to and protected against the poor. The poor in this context are seen as threats to society, the trouble rousers, and the disturbers of the peace of the society because of their poverty. They, therefore, cannot be catered to and protected on the same level as the rich and famous. The third layer to this assumption is when poverty, criminality, intellectual inferiority, and racial particularities are lumped into a single category to stigmatize a people.[88] The poor must be judged by the color of their skin, the

---

86. *American Sociological Review*, 2004, Vol. 69 (April: 151-169), Mass_ Imprisonment_ and _the _lif . . . e_Race_and_Class_Ineq[1].pdf. 156

87. Arthur L. Rizer 111, *The Race Effect On Wrongful Convictions*: Rizer Article formatted Current. Doc, 7_Rizer[1].pdf, *William Mitchell Law Review*, Vol. 29:3 p 848. (Susan H. Bitensky, Section 1983: Agent of Peace or Vehicle of Violence Against Children, 54 OKLA. L. Rev. 333, 372 n.61 (2001); Constance R. LeSage, The Death Penalty for Rape-Cruel and Unusual Punishment?, 38 LA. L. Rev. 868, 870 n.8 (1978).

88. Ibid. Rizer[1].pdf, *William Mitchell Law Review*, Vol. 29:3 p 848. p 857: There seems to be overwhelming evidence to prove that the system benefits the rich and famous to the demise of the poor and minority:

shape of their eyes, the texture of their hair, the spelling of their names, the intonation of their words, their intelligence, and their bank account.

No matter how petulant the differences are in view of our common humanity, they are exulted and distorted to define the destiny of a people. The materiality of the person becomes the immediate yardstick by which his destiny is decided. His physicality becomes the central organizing factor to his future. Physical features like nose, hair, mouth, skin, and body contours consciously become the ultimate paradigm to determine the validity of a person. They are buttressed by bad theological anthropology. Because white is good and black is bad, what is bad is dangerous and must be gotten rid of. Therefore if a human being is black, he or she is bad, and because he or she is a black human being, they must be treated with suspicion.

The effect of this form of consciousness about a people is detrimental. The claim that "badness" and criminality are associated with an entire group of people as a subconscious and conscious expression manifests itself in several ways. There are two forms of internalizations that take place in this regard. One is the internalization to be in control so that what is bad will not take control. The media flood the consciousness of the populace with criminalizing images of the black man. With no regard for objectivity and truth, one group must be presented as "bad" and the other group presented as "good." The "they" against "us" mentality is overtly and covertly displayed on

---

"The wealthy benefit from a criminal justice system that sends the message that it is the poor, not the rich, who commit crimes and whom the middle class, should fear. As a result of the criminal justice system's focus on street crime and not 'white collar' or environmental crime, it is the poor who seem a threat to the social order, not the rich; and this view reinforces the familiar American association between wealth and virtue, poverty and moral bankruptcy . . . 'if we can convince [society] that the poor are poor because of their own shortcomings, particularly moral shortcomings like incontinence and indolence, then we need acknowledge no . . . responsibility to the poor.' [the result is that] 'the ultimate sanctions of criminal justice dramatically sanctify the present social and economic order, and the poverty of criminal makes poverty itself an individual moral crime."

a daily basis in the media. As a result, a child grows up, especially a white child, with the mentality that the black man is a criminal. He or she grows up, and is given access to strategic power. With the hatred, suspicion, and negativity introduced into their little innocent minds and memories at such a tender age by the media or by other means, they assume leadership and perpetuate the cycle of hatred, suspicion, and negativity. But they have never had a personal encounter with a black person unless through the media. They went to high school in the suburb and went to a university or college where blacks make up 5% of the student population (or the lack thereof). They might not have had a black friend, or if they did, it was a mere acquaintance. They might never have had a black instructor or a black student in either their undergraduate or graduate classes. The immediate consequence is felt when such a person becomes a law enforcement officer. Their only encounter with a black person will be as a police officer. You can imagine how they might react. Don't forget that a black person can become submerged into a terrible race consciousness against other blacks by association since racism is also a consciousness that is to a large extent socially constructed and perpetuated.

The other form of internalization is the one concurrently taking place in the mind of the black person who is considered "bad" because he is black. He or she internalizes the projections that they are black and therefore something must be wrong with them. Especially for the young person who is often struggling with their sense of identity. A healthy family upbringing with positive role models and enforcement might minimize the effects of this internalization. On the other hand, the lack of a healthy family upbringing might enforce the internalization of the feeling that I am black and something is wrong with me. This internalization informs the interpretation of their reality of life, the construction and interpretation of meaning for survival. It leads to the distortion of who they are and their self-image. The only paradigm and lens that they can see through for the construction of meaning is a stereotyped paradigm. A stereotyped paradigm consists of a set of negative value systems externally imposed upon a social group of people and are racially, tribally, socially, religiously, culturally and politically demeaning. The danger is when a stereotyped paradigm is assumed as one's own: when I call myself a criminal, a thug, a nigger because society says I am a criminal, a nigger, and a thug.

The internalization of a stereotyped paradigm manifests itself in three ways: self-distortion, self-deception, and self-destruction. Self-distortion is expressed through the habit of accepting the stereotype that the majority imposes on the minority as their own. Self-deception is manifested in the assertion that one has internalized this consciousness to feel safe and secured but they are not. Self destruction takes place when the internalization of the stereotype has come to fruition and the individual assumes the identity of what he or she is struggling against. Yet all of these manifestations are experienced at several levels. It is felt in one's desire to progress and advance despite the odds, yet the frustration is experienced at having the doors slammed in your face because you are black. It is the agony a black intellectual and professional experiences when his qualifications or experience are trampled upon and his subordinate whom he trained and apprenticed is elevated above him because the apprentice is white. It is the despair experienced when society says to you, "you are no good" and "school is not good for you," and you must figure out something else to do and despair sets in. Despair is when you have come to the "end of your possibilities." In this context, it is initiated by a structure, a teacher, or a person in authority with the power to shape and reshape your potential for life. The structure has seemingly closed the door to your destiny and has opened another one. For most black students who go through this experience, without much inner strength to persevere, the frustration and disappointment are sometimes channeled through the life of the street.

Commenting on the reason for the so-called high crime rate among blacks in 1921, Du Bois argued that the black individual is perpetually viewed as a criminal with overt or covert suspicion wherever they go. The solution to the elimination of crime, Du Bois wrote, was training. He writes, "The chief problem in any community cursed with crime is not the punishment of the criminals but the preventing of the young from being trained to crime" (Du Bois: *The Relation of Negroes to Whites in the South*). The black person is caught in the circle of racial consciousness and assumptions, freedom, phenomenon of the color line, poverty, and stereotypes. Du Bois' emphasis on "training" and "prevention" contrasts Hegel's assertion that punishment as the fundamental means of correction is the negation of the right of the criminal to commit crime. Hegel as an enlightenment figure does not positively respond to the consciousness of racism and its sociopolitical and economic influence in the formulation of laws and policies.

He argues that "the criminal act . . . is itself negative, so that the punishment is merely the negation of the negation. Actual right is thus the cancellation [*Aufhebung*] of this infringement . . . ."[89] Punishment is the just cancellation of the criminal act. In this case, deterrence and reform are not relevant since punishment must oppose and cancel the abstract right to commit crime through the will in the concrete world. Punishment must come against the crime within the person since, according to Hegel, "crime in itself is an infinite injury"[90] to the one who commits a crime. In Hegel, we find a perpetual criminalization of the criminal; the notion that the criminal is inherently a criminal and so must be considered a criminal, a stigma he must live with for the rest of his life with little or no hope of breaking through.

According to Du Bois, the fundamental consciousness in the persecution of crime committed by a black person is first the "color of the criminal" rather than the crime itself. While he writes about crime and sees the persecution of crime as primarily influenced by the color line, Du Bois is optimistic that the problem of the color line can be resolved in America if both sides of the spectrum recognize

---

89. Hegel, PR. 97. "Through a crime, something is altered, and the thing [*Sache*] exists in this alteration; but this existence is the opposite of thing itself, and is to that extent within itself [in sich] null and void. The nullity is [the presumption] that right as right has been cancelled [*aufgehoben*]. For right, as an absolute, cannot be cancelled, so that the expression of crime is within itself null and void, and this nullity is the essence of the effect of crime. But whatever is null and void must manifest itself as such—that is, it must itself appear as vulnerable. The criminal act is not an initial positive occurrence followed by the punishment as its negation, but is itself negative, so that the punishment is merely the negation of the negation. Actual right is thus the cancellation [*Aufhebung*] of this infringement, and it is in this very circumstance that it demonstrates its validity and proves itself as a necessary and mediated existence [*Dasein*]."

90. Ibid., PR. 218, pg. 251. "Crime in itself is an infinite injury, but as an *existence* [*Dasein*], it must be measured in terms of qualitative and quantitative differences and since its existence is essentially determined as a *representation* [*Vorstellung*] and *consciousness of the validity of the laws*, its *danger is civil society* is a determination of its magnitude, or even one of its qualitative determinations."

LOCKED UP AND LOCKED DOWN

the need for change in attitude and perceptions. As an intellectual who was very objective and candid about his analyses, Du Bois could see the error on both sides of the spectrums for not desiring change and personal transformation. For him, the color line, manifested by "proscription and prejudice" undermines "thrifts and intelligence." On the other hand, blacks, he cautioned, are not to

> declare that color-prejudice is the sole cause of their social condition, nor for whites to reply that their social condition is the main cause for prejudice. They both act, as reciprocal, and a change in neither alone will bring the desired effect. Both must change, or neither can improve to any great extent.... Only by a union of intelligence and sympathy across the color-line in this critical period of the Republic shall justice and right triumph (Du Bois: *The Soul of Black Folk*).[91]

In summary, the statistics are scary but hope is not lost. The existential understanding of the black community's encounter with God has always been a pivotal source of strength and encouragement. I will now define the above statistics in view of what the Bible has to say about prison, the prisoner and the modern prison system. As a Christian endeavoring to derive solutions to the prevailing situation I believe adopting a biblical consciousness of humanity and crime will, to a large extent transform the present paradigm and prism by which we continue to define the black man in relation to crime and punishment.

[91.] W.E.B Du Bois, *The Souls of Black Folk* (New York: Dover Publication, INC, 1994), 113.

Chapter Three

What Does the Bible Say?

The Spirit of the Sovereign Lord is upon me, because the Lord has anointed me to preach good news to the poor. He has sent me to bind up the brokenhearted, to proclaim freedom for the captives and release from darkness for the prisoners.

—Isaiah 61:1

This analysis looks at Dr. Christopher Marshall's work on prison and the Bible. The thrust of his argument is that the Bible rejects imprisonment, condemns the modern prison system, does not condone the criminal as an inherent criminal and neither does it condone the racialization of crime or prison as an economic enterprise.

According to Marshall, the United States and New Zealand topped the chart for the highest amount of prison population in 2002. In 2009, the United States has the highest amount of those imprisoned in the world. According to the Washington Post-New High In U.S. Prison Numbers: "With more than 2.3 million people behind bars, the United States leads the world in both the number and percentage of residents it incarcerates, leaving far-more-populous *China* a distant second, according to a study by the nonpartisan *Pew Center*

LOCKED UP AND LOCKED DOWN

on the States." [92] More jails, more money spent more stringent measures, more people behind bars, and more association of crime with black men. According to the King James Version of the Bible, *prison* appears ninety times, *prisoner* thirteen times, and *prisoners* twenty times. Marshall asserts that most church folk don't want to know what is happening in the prisons and the consequences upon the community. They are happy that "criminals" are locked up. Once they are out of sight, they must be out of mind. According to Marshall, that is the problem because the Bible is about justice and not injustice, repentance and not reproach, rebuke and not hostility, forgiveness and not exclusion, restoration and not destruction.

He argues that the prison system we are accustomed to is a recent development in human history. Prisons prior to the eighteenth century were noninstitutional. According to Marshall, "prisons have served principally as holding tanks where offenders could be detained prior to trial or to the carrying out of the sentence of the court, such as execution, exile or enslavement, or until debts or fines had been paid."[93] There are exceptions in the Bible: King Jehoiachin spent thirty-seven years in the Babylonian prison (2 Kings 24:15, 25:2-7; Jer. 52:31-34); King Jehoahaz died in an Egyptian prison, not much is found on King Zedekiah after he was captured and jailed by the Babylonians (2 King 25:2-7; Jer. 39:1-7, 52:3-11).

The development of the modern prison system was viewed as a face-lift, a center for the reshaping, reforming, rehabilitating, and eventually restoring the individual to the society in contrast to the old

---

92.   Dr. Christopher D. Marshall, *Prison, Prisoners and the Bible* (A paper delivered to "Breaking Down the Walls Conference," Tukua Nga Here Kia Marama Ai, Matamata, 14-16 June, 2002 [Accessed. Feb. 2, 2009) p. 1.

93.   Ibid., 3.

94.   Ibid., 3 "Prior to this time, the system of punishment was largely arbitrary and often brutal. There was little proportionate gradation of penalties. The sanction imposed upon offenders depended largely on the whim of the magistrate or prince, and there was a much stronger emphasis on hurting the body, by torture, mutilation, the stocks or the gallows, than on reforming the mind or changing the character of the offender. But as the idea of rehabilitation took hold, it contributed considerably to mitigating the severity of criminal law. The function of imprisonment changed from being a system for detaining people before sentence to becoming a mode of punishment in its own right."

system. The old system in its treatment of prisoners was humiliating. What was, however intended to change the brutal system of torture and bodily harm became a penal system of punishing the soul and the body behind bars.[94] Yet this new system, with good intentions was initiated by the Church but became a tool for destruction. According to Marshall,

> what began as a humanitarian gesture has since become one of the most violent and inhumane institutions in modern society. Twice as many rapes, for example, take place inside US prison as are inflicted on women outside prison. Caging people for long periods of time, depriving them of autonomy and responsibility and self-respect, tearing apart their families, so that the innocent relatives and children of inmates suffer, throwing together dysfunctional and damaged people into a huge zoo, and all in [the] name of 'correcting' them, is both inhumane and counter-productive . . . . Nor is it a response to crime that can claim any biblical support whatsoever.[95]

Imprisonment was not a strange phenomenon to most of the individuals in the Bible. From the Old Testament to the New Testament, we see biblical characters going in and out of prison for various reasons. Joseph was sold into slavery and subsequently imprisoned on false accusations. Samson and Daniel were imprisoned for political reasons; the prophets were imprisoned for religious reasons; and finally, Peter, Paul, and other disciples were imprisoned for causing religious and social upheaval wherever they went with the preaching of the resurrected Christ.[96] For Paul, while at one time he was the one locking people up; after his conversion, he became a jailbird and was constantly locked up, for example in Philippi, Caesarea, and Rome, etc.,[97] so that he could take on the name "prisoner of Jesus Christ."[98] Perhaps that was the identity on the record for Paul. According to Marshall,

> prison is not the only criminal sanction cited in the New Testament. A whole variety of other judicial and extra-judicial *punishments*

---

95.   Ibid., 4.

96.   Acts 8:3, 9:1-2; 22:4-5; 26:10; Phil. 3:6.

97.   Acts 16:19-40, 23:10ff; 24:27; 28:16, 20, 30.

98.   Eph. 3:1; Philem. 1, 9, cf. 2.Tim 1:8.

LOCKED UP AND LOCKED DOWN

are also mentioned in passing, decapitation, drowning, hanging, precipitation, mutilation, stoning, excommunication, exile, chaining, putting in stock, scourging, sawing in two, torture (which came in many forms), and crucifixion. Quite often, the victims of such barbarities are not evildoers but those at the margins of mainstream Jewish and Greco-Roman society.[99]

The leaders of the first church had a recidivism rate that was high. But it was the gruesomeness of imprisonment, its impact on one's freedom and sense of personhood that on several occasions demanded the intervention of God in the Bible.

Marshall gives five reasons for imprisonment in biblical times: First, "imprisonment was a cause of great suffering."[100] For example, Jeremiah was dropped in a "cistern" and "dungeon where he remained for a long time" for prophesying that Jerusalem would go into captivity. He suffered greatly and, upon being released, begged not to be sent there again.[101] The prophet Micaiah was imprisoned and punished with starvation on a diet of just bread and water.[102] According to Marshall, prisons were associated with death, starvation, torture, suicide, etc.[103]

---

99. Christopher D Marshall, *Beyond Retribution: A New Testament Vision for Justice, Crime and Punishment* (Michigan, William B. Eerdmans Publishing Company 2001) P. 16 n.

100. Marshall *Prison, Prisoners and the Bible*, 4.

101. Jer. 38, 37

102. I Kings 22:27; 2 Chron. 18:26

103. Marshall, *Prison, Prisoners and the Bible* "The psalmist speaks of 'prisoners in misery and in irons,' captives who 'groan' and are 'doomed to die.' Job considers Sheol to be preferable to imprisonment, for at least there 'the prisoners are at ease together [and] do not hear the voice of the taskmasters.' Things were no better in New Testament times. With few exceptions, prisons in the Roman period were dark, disease-ridden, and overcrowded places. It was common for prisoners to die in custody, either from disease or starvation, brutal torture, execution, or suicide. Imprisonment is commonly described by ancient authors as a fate worse than death; even the thought of it was appalling." (Ps. 107:10, 79:11; 102:20; Job 3:18; Matt. 25:36; Matt. 18:34; Heb. 13:3; cf. Jer. 52:11; 2Chron. 16:10; Mark 6:14-29; Phil. 1:19-24).

Secondly, imprisonment in biblical times was viewed as "an instrument of oppression more than an instrument of justice."[104] With only one place where prison is considered a "judicial sanction" for unlawful behavior and, in this case, the refusal to abide by the king's decree and the law of God in the book of Ezra,[105] Marshall argues that "prison is not prescribed as a criminal sanction in the Old Testament Law" but subsequently introduced by Israel.[106] Prisons were introduced as a result of the "development of standing armies and military establishments."[107] Restitution, instead of retribution and imprisonment, was considered the most adequate means of dealing with the offender because the goal was "expressing repentance toward God."[108] Furthermore, the communal sense of Israel's social ethos made it difficult for wrongful actions to be considered as independent individual actions due to the belief that the consequences of an individual's action affected the entire community.[109] Furthermore, Israel's experience of slavery in Egypt could not allow prisons and imprisonment to be a legislated form of treatment for long terms. This was the reason why God told Moses to set aside six cities as Cities of Refuge for purposes of rehabilitation and reintroduction into the society even though the cities of refuge were for crimes committed accidentally. According to Marshall,

> Israel's experience of imprisonment in Egypt made an indelible mark on her national memory, and consequently on her social policy. Israel never forgot the bitterness of slavery, nor God's action of setting her free from servitude. Israel therefore never used enslavement as a form of criminal punishment. She *did* still practice a form of slavery, but never felt easy doing so, and the covenant law built into the institution had several limitations and humanitarian

---

104. Marshall, *Prison, Prisoners and the Bible,* P. 7
105. Ezra 7:26
106. Marshall, *Prison, Prisoners and the Bible,* P. 7
107. Ibid., 7
108. Ibid., 7
109. Ibid., 7

protections. Indeed in many ways Hebrew slavery was a more humane institution than modern imprisonment, for slaves were at least permitted to participate in normal family and community life.[110]

Long-term imprisonment instead was used for political and military purposes; for example, individuals of defeated armies and their leaders, disloyal leaders of the governing authorities, those captured for enslavement, the punishment of prisoners of war, and religious leaders as a result of religious persecutions.[111] While imprisonment was used to punish political dissidents, criminals, religious opposition, etc., the modern form of imprisonment has added two new dimensions: economic profitability and racial sentencing to a large extent enforced by a racial consciousness and the criminalization of the black man. The biblical analysis of prisoners and imprisonment does not mention an economic industry built on prisoners, neither a form of imprisonment and sentencing influenced and informed by racism. According to Marshall,

> Scriptures' consistently negative perspectives on imprisonment should alert us to the inherent tendency of all prison systems to oppress and abuse people in the name of some higher goal. This in turn should caution us against excessive or normative reliance on imprisonment as a means of dealing with wrongdoing, since the power to imprison can so easily become a mechanism of oppression.[112]

He goes on to argue that criminal justice cannot be totally devoid of social justice when those easily imprisoned are the economically poor, marginalized, victims of discrimination, deprived, and disadvantaged in the society. The tendency in this regard to sentence individuals for longer prison term takes the focus from "the real causes of crime—which are as much to do with social circumstances as with

---

[110.]   Ibid., 8

[111.]   Ibid., 8

[112.]   Ibid., 8.

individual wickedness."[113] Marshall argues that the Bible's idea of imprisonment is different from that of the modern prison industry. He writes, "The criminal justice system can oppress as well protect; it can persecute as well as punish. Once again, the alertness of the biblical tradition to this fact should caution against a naive trust in the capacity of the cage to conquer sin."[114]

The third reason for imprisonment in the Bible according to Marshall is the identification of prisons with "the spirit and power of death."[115] Imprisonment in this context implies a spiritual reality of death: separation and estrangement. Furthermore, instead of imprisonment being used to bring humanity closer to one another, it is utilized to divide. In prison, new criminal behaviors are acquired, and old ones are often enhanced as first-term offenders are lumped together with hardened criminals. According to Marshall, "plain common sense should tell us that we will never defeat violence by throwing nonviolent people together within a violent environment,

---

[113]   Ibid., 9. "Under certain social conditions people will turn to crime who in other social climates would remain law-abiding. Poverty, unemployment, racial inequality, social prejudice, family dysfunction, and drug and alcohol abuse all have a role in fostering crime. A significant proportion of criminal offenders have been offended against as children before they become offenders. It is crucial rather than being content to divide individuals into categories of guilty and innocent and tossing the guilty into jail. Society's own complicity in the creation of criminals, is quickly lost sight of in the outpouring of moral indignation at individual offenders. It is also important to recognize that the law which criminals break is not a neutral transcription of absolute morality. It is an irrefutable fact, Barbara Hudson insists, that the law is predominantly reflective of the standpoint of the powerful, property-owning, white male and that the justice system bears down more heavily on the poor and disadvantaged than on the rich and the powerful. One recent study in New Zealand shows how the government puts far more money and resources into cracking down on welfare benefit fraud than on white collar crime, even though the cost of white collar crime and corporate fraud is up to 10 times higher than the cost of all other crimes combined."

[114]   Ibid., 10.

[115]   Ibid., 10.

especially in light of what has been called 'the contagious nature of criminality.'"[116] Prisons therefore lead to anxiety, meaninglessness, and hatred. The biblical solution, which reveals the mind of God, seeks to liberate the prisoner by "setting the captive free, opening prison doors" rather than the construction for economic gain.[117]

Marshall's fourth reason argues that "God wants to set prisoners free." The Bible does not endorse imprisonment. Imprisonment is biblically viewed as means of injustice, oppression, and the spirit of death. Prison is viewed negatively in the Bible and only serves as an opportunity for God's divine deliverance. Marshall argues that this negative evaluation of prison provides a premise for God as the one who wants to set the captive free and to break the chains of bondage. The psalmist speaks of a God who "looks down from his holy height, from heaven . . . to hear the groans of the prisoners, to set free those who were doomed to die." The same God who "made heaven and earth, the sea, and all that is in them," the same God who "executes justice for the oppressed [and] gives food to the hungry" is also the God who "set the prisoners free."[118]

In Luke 4:16-20, Jesus, Marshall argues, was not simply interested in spiritual and psychological liberation but liberation from "material structures and ideological systems which robbed them of freedom and dignity."[119] Freedom, in the biblical sense, according to Marshall has "both external and internal dimensions."[120] In the Old Testament, freedom is viewed as liberation from "external constraints (poverty, debt, slavery, oppressions, and military oppression)." The New Testament on the other hand emphasizes an "*interior* moral and spiritual freedom which the Christian gospel brings, a freedom from demons and despair, from sin and selfishness, from guilt and greed."[121] One can therefore argue that the biblical notion of freedom is holistic and contradicts the modern form of imprisonment and vengeful

---

[116]. Ibid., 10.

[117]. Ibid., 11.

[118]. Ibid. 11 Deut. 7:8; 24:18; Pss. 68:6, 79: 11;102:10-16; 118:5; 146:7; Isa. 427; 45:13; 49:13; 49:8-9; 61:1;; Micah 6:4; Zech. 9:11; Acts 5:19; 16:25-26; 1Pet. 3:19; Rev. 2:10, Pss. 102: 19, cf. 79:11, 146: 6-7

[119]. Ibid., 12.

[120]. Ibid., 12.

[121]. Ibid., 12.

penology as Muelder argues. The underlining reason for the Bible's opposition to the modern form of imprisonment and the penal system is that it categorically undermines God's holistic plan and purpose for the human being. There is no biblical justification for imprisonment based on race and the profit margin.

This holistic understanding of freedom as pivotal to Jesus' ministry is evident in the Gospels. Salvation in this regard does not only cater to the spiritual and interior estrangement of the human being but to their external and psychosocial estrangement in the concrete realm of human sociopolitical and economic activities. It is with this mindset that we can only understand and be sensitive to the prevailing rate of incarceration and detention of black men. To reiterate, the Bible does not mention or hint at a racial motive for incarcerating prisoners neither do we find any argument for prisons and detention facilities as industrial complexes for economic gains. According to Marshall, even if these forms of imprisonment and sentencing practices were present, they would fall under the category of human oppression, thus necessitating God's divine intervention and deliverance. Marshall's analysis also raises another point of contention: our perception about the other person and how we relate to them. As evident in the analysis, racial and criminalizing assumptions as instruments of justice undermine the nature of justice and leads to an ontological distortion of the human being. It is in this context that we can adequately understand the debilitating feeling of racially informed and influenced detention and incarceration as it generates questions concerning the worth and inherent dignity of any person.

I conclude this section with the testimony of Bro. Steve Johnson. I met Stevee at Morning Star Baptist Church in Boston and knew that there was a transformative moment in his life. He had a testimony, and the result was a dramatic transformation of his life and lifestyle. Stevee's conversion experience captures the ethos of this work in several ways. It is my prayer that the reader will read Stevee's testimony as a prism through which the thrust of this book is revealed: the transformative power of God—the God above, the God between, and the God below who intervenes on behalf of those who cry out to him. While transformation may be affected sometimes by the susceptibilities of the human nature, the authentic encounter with God and the transformative moment experienced remains a guarantee for consistent growth and development into the nature of God through Christ Jesus.

> Turn upon yourself and be fine
> Turn upon yourself and be refined
> Turn upon yourself and be defined
> Turn upon yourself and be firmed
> The you that is fine is the you refined
> For the you that you find is the you affirmed
> Since the you defined is the you that is fine
> Turn upon yourself and be fine

(George Walters-Sleyon)

Stevee Johnson: "My Story from Gangster to God"

I was born in a small town called Nashville in Georgia, outside of Atlanta. I had three brothers and four sisters. We were a family with issues.

I saw my father constantly beat my mother for our over twenty-five years. As result of this, most of my brothers and sisters moved away from home early at the ages of fifteen and sixteen. I was the baby, and I had to stay home and witness everybody leave. Around the age of six or seven, I witnessed my father continue to beat my mother as usual. On one occasion, when my father was beating our mother, my oldest brother went to help my mother. He began to beat my father. My father ran into the house to get his 12-gauge shotgun and shot my brother Robert in the leg. Back in the '60s and '70s, the EMTs were slow. When my brother finally made it to the hospital, his leg was amputated, but he ended up bleeding to death.

As a result of this experience, I lost all sense of emotion. Hatred grew in my heart. I began to hate both men and women. I eventually began to hate people. With this, I began to grow up very mad and angry as I continued to watch my father get drunk and beat my mother every weekend. I began to hate the weekends because I knew my father would be getting drunk and subsequently beat my mother. This impacted my upbringing as I grew up with lots of hatred and bad temper, which I also transferred into my schooling.

At school, I was always fighting since I didn't have peace in my home. Unfortunately, we never went to church. I grew up having no clue about who Jesus Christ is. As I grew older, my only thought was to get some money and leave my home area. At the age of fourteen, I caught my first aggravated assault charge. Because of my temper, I was sent immediately to a boy's correctional facility. I did approximately two years there. But at the facility, I was also surrounded by other young men with the same issues, no real father and no clue about Jesus. Unfortunately, we learned more evil ways from one another than anything good, and furthermore, no one came to visit me for two years. I was released on the sixth month before my sixteenth birthday. At this point in my life, I had become strongheaded and would not listen to anyone.

At sixteen, I stole my first motorcycle. I was caught and sent back into lockup. I got out on my eighteenth birthday. While in jail, I learned the art of selling drugs. Still no one mentioned Jesus Christ to me, and furthermore, my family didn't attend church. At this point, my life was quickly turning for the worst and out of control. At eighteen, I was in my first high speed chase and stand off with the police. Between the drugs charges, possession of guns and money, I was given seven years in the State's prison system. I had never been locked up like that before in my entire life.

While in prison, I became even more violent because my experience from my previous imprisonment taught me that, in prison, you have to earn your respect. I learned how to beat people down in the prison. On my first day of entering the State Prison, as I entered my bunk and tried to relax, one of the prisoners, who was also notoriously known, came to claim me. We entered into a fight. The police guards came, and in the process of separating us, they hit me terribly at the back of my head, and blood began to ooze out. I become unconscious and fainted. I was given thirty-two stitches while in lockup. Thinking about it, I should have sued the police for treating me as such, but I was ignorant of my rights and I had a bad temper. Yet it was in self-defense because the underlining culture was that he came to try me to see if he could subdue me.

I did three years in prison and paroled out at twenty-one. With no better education and career or family to return to, while on parole, I ended up hustling and selling drugs, robbing people, and had no clue as to what it meant to be a man. I had not heard about Jesus Christ, and no one from the church even approached me to share the gospel. So from twenty-one onward, I sold drugs, slept with women after women from city to city. I went from Miami to Cleveland, Ohio, from New York to Atlanta, and back to Miami. I kept on trafficking cocaine from Miami to Atlanta to Jacksonville, Florida. My clientele included blacks and whites, businessmen, lawyers, professionals, nonprofessionals, hustlers, addicts, and pimps. Because of my business and business connections, I came to own several cars, my own house yet with no peace of mind, no love, and no future.

At this point in my life, I was sniffing cocaine and gambling. In 1991, I was shot in my left arm from a drive-by shooting. But my life was spared, and yet I could not turn to God. I became even more of a gangster and worst in my pursuit. However, something happened that made me lose everything that I had. I came to the end of my life, and I was hopeless. I found myself homeless in Atlanta with my two daughters and reduced down to nothing. I was troubled.

It was then that I was able to hear from God. I began to repent to God at this time, but I didn't know that I was repenting. I was only asking God if he would raise me up and make me the man that he wants me to be, I will never turn away from the gospel. When I said that, I had no clue as to what I was saying, but instantly peace came into my heart and I had such a burning desire to know this God of the Bible.

From August 18 of 1996 to this day, God has changed my life, has blessed my soul, and has given me a charge to keep. So I must tell the world that Jesus Christ saves no matter who you are and where you have been. The gospel of Jesus Christ is for every woman, man, child, whomsoever. Yes, I may have a CORI, but I also have a conscience; I may have a record, but I also have redemption, my mess became my message. Now I work with teenage boys to help point them to truth and righteousness.

*   *   *

Stevee is now a pastor with a ministry in Atlanta, Georgia. He goes around preaching the Word of God. He completed his GED and got some formal training in working with young people and has worked with the Department of Youth Services in the Boston area.

Chapter Four

Am I Worthy as I Am?

It's a feeling of despisal,
A feeling of rejection
It's a feeling of not being a part
Of the whole
It's a feeling of the other
A feeling of distortion
It's a feeling of a disconnect
Of the soul
      Am I worthy as I am?
      Am I worthy ask I Lord
      Am I worthy as a person?
Should be taken as they are
You see the staring of the eyes
The hasting of the footsteps
You see the distance that is made
Because of you
It's a struggle for acceptance
A struggle to participate
A struggle to accommodate
You and I

Am I worthy as I am?
Am I worthy ask I Lord
Am I worthy as a person?
Should be taken as they are
Why should I feel this way?
Why should I feel this way?
This stereotype feeling
This stereotype guilt on my mind
Can anybody help me?
Can anybody tell me?
Can anybody hear me cry?
The anguish of rejection
Why . . . ?Why . . . ?Why . . . ?

—George Walters-Sleyon

Ontological distortion is any treatment that negates and reduces the inherent worth of a person. It is that which defines a person strictly on material and physical grounds, thus undermining and reducing the essential nature of a person to what is secondary. Racially motivated arrest, sentencing, detention, and incarceration lead to ontological distortion of self because it is racially motivated. In that case the racialized person is forced to consistently question their sense of selfhood because society has categorized them as secondary. They inquire: where did I come from? (sense of origin), who am I? (sense of identity), what is wrong with me? (sense of alienation), why am I here? (sense of meaning), and where am I going? (sense of destiny). These questions speak of hopelessness and meaninglessness characterized by alienation and agony. Over a million black men in their cells in prisons, jails, and detention or correction facilities on their bunk beds around the country ask themselves these questions on a daily basis. Those in detention for deportation are baffled by the lack of explanation for their lack of release or deportation. Those in jails are baffled by the relationship between the trivialization of who they are in the sentencing process and the crime they have committed or didn't commit. Both the black detainee and the black prisoner share some things in common: their African origin and blackness, the stereotype associated with their blackness, and the criminalization of their blackness. Both have lost their freedom, and with the prevailing statistics highlighting the frequency with which they are arrested, detained, and incarcerated, both share an inescapable fate: racialization, criminalization, and suspicion.

In this chapter, I want to theologically analyze the consciousness that criminalizes and the assumptions associated with the racialized form of incarceration as issues that conflict with the knowledge of God. An anthropology that promotes the consciousness of essential superiority of one group of people and the essential inferiority of another group of people based on race, color, and physicality eventually leads to the construction of a theological consciousness that promotes such claims. Bad theology leads to bad anthropology, and bad anthropology leads to bad theology since an individual's theology often influences their anthropology, i.e., one's consciousness of God often influences their consciousness of humanity. If theology reflects the way in which we have experienced God and the understanding and knowledge derived from that experience is used to inform our social relationships and practices, then our anthropology or how we perceive other human beings is highly influenced and informed by our theology. If not, then we are deliberately implementing a strange dichotomy or divide between our theology and how we perceive others so as to avoid accountability and live a life of cognitive dissonance.

The situation of over one million men of African descent and ancestry incarcerated and detained concerns us, and it should concern us holistically as Christians in every objective way. This is not a thesis on theology but a narrative with theological implications. The situation deserves a theological understanding because it affects us as human beings, not only physical beings but ontological beings whose sense of self is threatened with the experience of nonbeing. The threat of nonbeing implies the devaluation of a human being. Nonbeing in it's nature is that which militates against being. This devaluation says to the human beings, "You are an object"; and because you are an object, you are devoid of feelings, reactions as a normal human being, responses, and other forms of attributes associated with "real" human beings.

The threat of nonbeing to being expresses itself in this context either subtly or overtly in the form of racial depersonalization. It feels like living on the fringes or on the fence, always a part of the whole but never becoming members of the whole. A member of the whole exists with the self-confidence and assurance of accommodation by other members of the whole, as equals and worthy of contribution and benefits, as participants in the structural and institutional makeup of the whole that is expected of every member of the whole who is accepted. This is followed by a sense of acceptance by the whole to be secured of one's membership, protected from other members who may threaten the membership of others.

Living as such for the black person is concrete and nonconcrete. It is nonconcrete in the sense that it affects the existence of the individual, a people, a community, and a group. It is therefore theological in the sense that knowledge of the total reliance on the "Ground" of their being is sought in the struggle against the threatening use of race, skin color, hair texture, body contours, spelling and sound of one's name, etc., as the sole lense through which policies are constructed, realities are interpreted, and meanings are constructed. The effect for the black person upon their sense of being is felt beyond the physicality of who they are into the interiority of their being. Yet the one who sees only the deemed and material reflection of skin color and all forms of physicality either consciously knows he or she is inflicting pain or is subconsciously acting out on impulses buried in the storehouse of their memory: the interiority of their being.

The effect is directed at the "essence" of the person who is of African descent. Their blackness is socially pathological and therefore must not be encouraged in certain respects. It is considered a negation and therefore must be resisted. The worst fear in this social milieu for a nonblack person is to wake up in the morning, look in the mirror, and realize they are black, their hair turned "kinky," commensurate with a black body. At this, they might scream, "I am doomed, and beauty is doomed." On the reverse, a black person who wakes up in the morning and discovers that he or she has been transformed into a white person might think, "I have arrived." But why should we think like this? Is it not because of what blackness has come to symbolize and what black people are made to represent while whiteness and lightness has come to symbolize wealth, status, beauty, privilege, etc? We are afraid to become what we have created because we see the consequences of what we have made, and it is threatening to us. Blackness is devalued and black human beings criminalized. We have psychologically conditioned our minds to think that any being other than us is an inferior being, and we cannot be reduced to the status of inferior beings because inferiority connotes criminality and the entity of nonbeing. As a result of this sociopsychological conditioning of our minds, we have redefined and reduced the "image of God," an ontological nature in every human being to a domesticated category. We have in essence distorted what God has made "good" by conditionalizing and qualifying it. This distortion by human beings against other human beings is the greatest harm done to humanity by humanity. Its effect is felt in the corridors of academia; the confines of media rooms, in the cradles of public policy formulation, in the balance of justice and the board rooms of economic institutions where life defining decisions are made on a daily basis.

We are conscious of the fact that the use of the knowledge of God to assert our superiority is totally inconsistent with the nature of God, but we perpetrate and condone it because of the sociopolitical and economic benefit and privilege it accrues for us. It is sin, but we must tolerate it. We do not want to talk about it because it will convict us. Since conviction leads to transformation and accountability, we'd rather not talk about it. We do not want to be confronted with the inconsistency of what we believe about the knowledge and nature of God and what we practice. We have postulated a cognitive dissonance of ontological magnitude and have allowed it to enter into who we are. We know that our anthropology is as a result of our theology, and if we have developed a bad anthropology, it is because we have developed a bad theology. Why should a particular group of people languish in prison, their families destroyed, their men and boys given distorted and twisted images about themselves while their wives and mothers weep for them? Where is the shared sense of human feeling, empathy, and identification? But we have hardened our hearts and refused to feel the pain and see the scars. We have denied that such pains and scars really exist. We do not want to be accountable, but deep in our consciousness we are aware that such pain and scars do exist, some we have caused, some we have influenced, and some self-inflicted.

The distortion of the understanding of the image of God as the spark of the divine in every human being and it's perpetuation through structural and institutional practices is also a major theological problem. It is a theological problem that every sincere Christian and preacher of the gospel of Jesus Christ must confront. While this distortion has accrued sociopolitical and economic privileges for some and their descendents, it has generationally deprived others and their descendents and consigned them to a life of generational impoverishment. This ontological devaluation of other human beings, thus the defiling of the spark of divinity in them, complicates the notion of estrangement for people who are racially marginalized. As human beings collectively estranged from God because of The Fall, the racially marginalized persons feel a second sense of estrangement. This estrangement is even more profound in his or her existential experience than the spiritual estrangement because it is concrete and immediate. He or she as a racially marginalized person must not only feel the burden of this ontological distortion of self but also endures a sociopolitical and economic marginalization and its attending consequences. They must continuously face the struggles of overcoming this subject/object distinction of self. This "twoness" of the self: How they perceive themselves as subjects with feelings, emotions, needs, wants, desires, ambitions, aspirations, and dreams often contradicts how the outside world, the sociopolitical milieu, and others perceive them as objects.

The society's racial perception of them establishes the lenses through which they are perceived. Their identity and aspirations, their dreams, are abandoned and their destiny clouded by society's racial consciousness while they silently weep on the inside. Oftentimes, they do not know that they are weeping because they have become used to their painful experience. Yet their pain is manifested in their sighing, etc. They weep not with tears in their eyes but with tears on the plates of their hearts and on the walls of their souls. They have wept so much, and since no one hears them, they have become one with their tears. When you see them, you feel them; when you hear them, you know them; when they sing, it is couched in the melodies of their songs, the beat of their rhythm, and the cadence of their tempo because there are tears on their music and they are weeping. Only the one who seeks to understand the shared mutuality of human connectedness will feel the pulsating beats of tears dropping gently in latent agony.

This contradiction of self in the society and self-negotiation in the world is a daily activity. The racially marginalized person is constantly negotiating their friends both racially and intra-racially. The reason is racially marginalized persons have different perceptions and experiences. They are involved with constantly negotiating their lives, negotiating their existence, their geographical location to soften the sharpness of their sociopolitical and economic marginalization. Their felt experience is existential because it often concerns their sense of personhood.[122] They are in the "world" but in some way "above the world" in their experience. They are above the world, and they are in the world because the world is not for them. Yet they are bound to the world and must negotiate their existence in this world. This is not like what Jesus said with respect to his mission. Jesus' articulation of this understanding was in reference to the coming of the Holy Spirit who was to be the helper of the believer living in the "world's system." The marginalized person on the other hand is negotiating an existential understanding of the world based on his or her sociopolitical and economic experience, based on how they are perceived, accepted, and accommodated by the concrete world. The racially marginalized person is thrown out of the world because of the social ethos of his social location. He must therefore often find ways of negotiating in this world to exist. Their social estrangement is more glaring than their spiritual estrangement. The marginalized person has a self-consciousness that is very intuitive. It is a social consciousness that is first existential because of the felt experience of the pain of marginalization. This consciousness is introspectively intuitive because they find themselves in immediate contact with the source of their

---

[122]   Paul Tillich, *Systematic Theology. Vol. One* (London, The University of Chicago Press, 1951) 175: "The individual is a person in the sight of the law. The original meaning of the word persona, (*prosopon*) points to the actor's mask which makes him a definite character. Historically . . . Personal standing has been denied to slaves, children, women. They have not attained full individualization in many cultures because they have been unable to participate fully; and, conversely, they have not been fully individualized. No process of emancipation was begun until the stoic philosophers fought successfully for the doctrine that every human being participates in the universal logos. The uniqueness of every person was not established until Christian churches acknowledged the universality of salvation and the potentiality of every human being to participate in it. This development illustrates the strict interdependence of individuality and participation on the level of complete individualization, which is, at the same time, the level of complete participation. The individual participated in his environment or, in the case of the complete individualization, in his world."

being. Instead of constantly turning outward and outside for hope and strength, they must turn inward and inside. They look within to find the "Ground of their being."

The black person has become experienced in knowing himself or herself especially in the West. He or she knows where to go and where not to go. This is not because of the feeling of inferiority and social dislocation but because of the felt sense of rejection and suspicion they are intuitively conscious of. As a result, they must return to the person within that prefigures the person on the outside. This is a constant activity, but the one who perpetuates rejection does not know.

The question about self and identity is one that has been around for centuries. But this question for the black person is important because it borders on skin color and race as the fundamental means of human identity. Is there another response that establishes human identity and selfhood beyond the realm of race and skin color? St. Augustine's response to this question is poignant. He answers affirmatively that there is ground for self-certainty that transcends racial and material identity. A distorted self-image and self-certainty can only be healed when one has gotten hold of a consciousness of self that transcends the material, that esteems the material in light of the immaterial. Such an understanding does not take its basic foundation from the material self but the immaterial self. For it is only when the immaterial self informs the material self can one's sense of selfhood be firmly established. The black child growing up in a society that has criminalized him before he comes to the consciousness of who he is must be told about who he really is, the one he does not see but is known by him.

It is in this context that St. Augustine's search for the authentic person is relevant, one that negates our prevailing consciousness of humanity. For St. Augustine, certainty about self and the confidence associated with self-certainty is grounded in God. It is therapeutic, rehabilitating, and transformative. Presented in St. Augustine's analysis of self-certainty is a fundamental argument against the racialization of the person and one's certainty of self. As a theological analysis, St. Augustine's analysis of self-certainty is an outright negation of Hegel's assertion of the criminal as inherently a criminal in the concrete world. Theologically, Hegel's notion of crime and punishment refuses to see any possibility of a second chance for the criminal in the political world. This view of crime and punishment reflects the existential angst of the black man who commits a crime. Hegel's theory becomes particularly problematic when a racial consciousness is taken into consideration. St. Augustine differs from Hegel in that Augustine upholds the inherent worth of the person as created in the image of God. He does not see the sinner as totally depraved; neither is the criminal inherently a criminal. Since the inherent worth of the person is divine, Augustine presents a definition of the person in relation to God who provides a "second chance" for the criminal in the concrete world of sociopolitical and economic activities, thus rejecting Hegel's criminalization of the person. But for Augustine, this understanding of the other is derived from an understanding of self that is grounded in God.

St. Augustine

"What is self-certainty"? Augustine asked. How can I be certain that I am without appealing to material things or social status as the only source of my identity? Is self-certainty possible, and how can it be attained? These were some of the "vexing" questions that one of the greatest bishops Africa has produced struggled with. St. Augustine, Bishop of Hippo in North Africa (AD 354-430), embarked upon answering this question during his long career as a philosopher, a theologian, a writer, and a leader of the Church in Africa. In the writings of this great African Bishop, we see a notion of self-certainty through the soul and its activities that not only seeks to ground human rational understanding of self in God, but an ontological understanding that in Augustine's view, precedes one's racial justification of self and the other. Augustine's goal was to produce an understanding of self by referencing an interior understanding of self based on one's relationship with God.[123] For Augustine, there is a certainty of self that is first grounded not only on the five senses but also on the intelligible knowledge of God.

Self-certainty for Augustine is a consciousness, and this consciousness is of God within the consciousness of self. The soul that is ruled by God has the ability to rule the body. But never should the

---

[123.]   Edger Brightman, *Moral Law;* Plato was the first to assert an interior relationship in knowledge between the spiritual and physical world, 125·

soul succumb ultimately to the body, its appetites, and desires, for then the soul will find itself under the control of the body. God as superior should rule the soul and not the "inferior," which is the body.[124] The more the soul finds intimacy with God, the more it comprehends the body and true self-certainty. For Augustine, submission to God is the path to deliverance, the path to "truth and happiness," to "achieve perfect mental health." To know God is to know self. This certainty and "beauty," he argues is given only to those who enjoy the contemplation of God's eternal nature, to be moved and adorned by it, and to be able to merit eternal life."[125]

In Augustine's analysis, knowledge about the soul leads to the knowledge of God. The soul is spiritual and the body is physical. In establishing a major distinction between the soul and the material world, Augustine explains that he makes no "affirmation about the soul now except that it has come from God in such a way that it is not the substance of God and that it is incorporeal, that is, that it is not a body but a spirit."[126] The soul is immaterial, incorporeal, and spiritual. Even at death, the soul does not die.

In explaining the role of the soul in relation to self, Augustine argues that the soul has victory over the material world. The soul implies the totality of the human being, yet the soul and the body are one. He writes, "Whoever wishes to separate the body from human nature is a fool."[127] While the soul is naturally attracted to the body according to Augustine, "the soul seems to me to be a substance having rationality, which is fitted to the body to rule it."[128] Therefore "man . . . is a rational soul using a mortal and earthly body."[129] In *On the Trinity* (400-416), he speaks definitively, "Man is a rational substance made

---

[124.] *On Music,* VI, 5, 12-13; (Trans. Tafford P. Maher, S.J:, *The De Musica* VI of St. Augustine, Translated and Philosophically Annotated (St.Louis University Master's Thesis, 1939), 87-89.

[125.] *The True Religion,* 3.3; (trans. C.A. Hangartner, S.J., *De vera religione* (Chapters 1-17) (St. Louis University Master's Thesis, 1945), pp. 9, 11. 126 Eugene Portalie, *A Guide To The Thought of Saint Augustine* (Chicago, Henry Regnery Company 1960). 146

[127.] Ibid., 147.

[128.] Ibid. 147.

[129.] Ibid., 147.

up of soul and body . . . Man is, as the ancients said, a rational, mortal animal."[130]In essence, Augustine in this analysis is establishing the grounds for a coherent understanding of the person as a unit, holistic as body and soul, and intricately united.[131] The union of the soul and body for Augustine is a very intricate union that provides life and being to the body. He writes, "The body therefore subsists through the soul

---

[130]   Ibid., 147.

[131]   Kelly Brown Douglas W*hat's Faith Got to Do with It* (New York, Orbis Bookis, 2005) 19-18. In reflecting on the root of the social stereotypes defining people of African descent in America, Kelly Brown Douglas in her book: *What's Faith Got to Do with It* poignantly analyzes the root of racism as the fundamental cause for how Black people are perceived. According to Douglas, the enslavement and lynching of black people among prominent causes in America could be attributed to the division between the body and the soul predominant in Western philosophy and influenced by Rene Descartes. She argues that the American church was able to condone slavery and participate in the lynching of black bodies because Douglas argues, whites at the time believed that black bodies dualistically were highly inferior to white bodies. Secondly, since salvation was mainly concerned with the soul and not the body, blacks were prevented from baptism by white churches in the days of slavery and lynching. The understanding was that if blacks were baptized, they would be considered Christians and their souls saved. To save the black soul meant accommodating and accepting the black person as a person like any other white person and not enslaving, racializing or lynching them. Therefore, Douglas argues, to justify the lynching of black people, to keep them enslaved and racialized, the Church prevented black people from baptism, from the Eucharist and the preaching of the gospel. In that case, their bodies could be lynched and their souls unsaved. These were some of the reasons for the rebellion of black ministers to organize the Black Church. "In theological understanding, dualism connotes a particular kind of relationship. It commonly refers to an oppositional/antagonistic way of relating. In a dualistic relationship mutuality of difference is precluded. Dualistic paradigm places contrasting objects or elements into hostile and /or hierarchical overpowered, dominated, or not respected by the other. One element is typically revered while the other is vilified; one is considered good and the other evil."

LOCKED UP AND LOCKED DOWN

and exists by the very fact that it is animated . . . The soul gives form to the body so that the latter is body insofar as it exists."[132] He writes that "the body and soul are one man although the body and the soul are not one . . ."[133] To love God is to live above the passions of the body but not to abandon the body since we exist in the concrete world. For Augustine, the soul must maintain its spirituality. The union between the soul and the body is spiritual and mystical, which no human being can understand. The soul is indistinguishable from the body because they are one.[134] He argues that a better understanding of the soul leads to a better understanding of self.

Augustine establishes the spiritual understanding of self-certainty as a basis for the interior life and the physical life. For Augustine, this is the ground of selfhood, of personhood, and true self-identity. This is the true ground for human identity. It transcends the material body, for the material body cannot be all there is about the human being. To derive selfhood simply based on the material is to deny true identity to self. It is a recipe for subjugation and ill-treatment because the person is more than what the eye beholds. To find God is to look within one's soul where a seeker also finds the happy life. In his quest, Augustine inquires,

> How then am I to seek for you, Lord? When I seek for you, my God, my quest is for the happy life. I will seek you that 'my soul may live,' for my body derives life from my soul, and my soul derives life from you. How then shall I seek for the happy life? It is not mine until I say: "It is enough, it is there."[135]

This search for Augustine underscores his argument that the human being is made in the image of God with a spiritual self called the soul that establishes the identity of every human being. Augustine must look within himself to find himself. As he turns away from what he was doing that turned him away from God, in himself, he finds God, and the ground of who he is. He writes,

---

[132.] Portalie., 147.

[133.] Ibid., 147.

[134.] Ibid., 148

[135.] St. Augustine, *Confessions* (Trans. Henry Chadwick, Oxford, Oxford University Press, 1991) Book V11: X (16).

> With you as my guide I entered into my innermost citadel (himself) and was given power to do so because you had become my helper. I entered and with my soul's eye, such as it was, saw above that same eye of my soul the immutable light higher than my mind—not the light of every day, obvious to anyone . . . It was not that light, but a different thing, utterly different from all our kind of light . . . It was superior because it made me, and I was inferior because I was made by it. The person who knows the truth knows it, and he who knows it knows eternity . . . When I first came to know you, you raised me up to make me see that what I saw is Being, and that I who saw am not yet Being. And you gave a shock to the weakness of my sight by the strong radiance of your rays I trembled with love and awe. And I found myself far from you "in the region of dissimilarity," and heard as it were your voice from on high: "I am the food of the fully grown; grow and you will feed on me. And you will not change me into you like the food your flesh eats, but you will be changed into me."[136]

Augustine has stumbled upon something that he cannot "comprehend." The source of who he really "is" is immaterial. But Augustine is aware that in the process of deriving true self-identity, he must return to the material, to the body, because the body is not an enemy of self; both exist holistically. According to Augustine, possessing this understanding of self is self-liberating. It is liberating for the individual who comes to the consciousness of this knowledge and also perceives others as such. It is this notion of the human being as ontological and holistic that racism, and racialization, have distorted and subverted for sociopolitical, sociocultural, religious, and economic gains and empowerment. The result is the demoralization of other human beings, their perpetual subjugation to inhuman treatments and stereotypes, and their denial to participate in the process of human flourishing and the common good. Not only do we see in Augustine an adequate definition of selfhood but the lack of this understanding of self can only lead to the internalization of what society says about you and what society perpetuates about you. It is in this context that

---

136. Ibid., Book X: xix (29)

we see a lot of black youths internalizing several of the negative images about self that deny their true sense of being. The consequence, if one is not careful, is to manifest the internalized images in ways that are incompatible to their true self. Stereotypes are socially constructed, socially promoted, and fundamentally influential in the formulation of policies, the construction of meaning, and identity. The images they promote ultimately result in the objectification of the other person and their reduction to thinghood. It is in this context that we can understand the high rates of arrest, detention, and incarceration of black men and its social implications.

Self-certainty is within, its ground is divine. The human being is profound. The profundity of the human being as a person is not based on black or white, brown or yellow, pink or blue, money or no money, food or no food, education or no education, job or no job, criminal or noncriminal, offender or no offender, victim or no victim, but because the person simply "is." Augustine's theological analysis of self-certainty rejects the consciousness that racializes the other person, thus reducing them to "thinghood." For Augustine, the person simply "is"—an ontological being of inherent worth and dignity. It is a negation of Hegel's criminalization of the criminal: the claim that crime defines the criminal's essential worth. For Hegel, the criminal will always be a criminal because crime once committed defines the criminal's identity and essentially stigmatizes them in the concrete world of sociopolitical activities. For St. Augustine: "All have sinned and fallen short of the glory of God, and are justified freely by God's grace through the redemption that came by Christ Jesus. God presented him as a sacrifice of atonement through faith in his blood" (Romans 3:23-25).

The Groundless Me`

I must return to myself and find me`
The me` of myself in me
Since the me you see needs me`
   I shall relinquish myself to furnish me`
   The me` of groundless me`
   Since the me you need is me`
   -the groundless me`
I will respond to the me` in me
The myself of me`

Since the me` of me is myself
Reduce me not to the me you see
For the me you see needs me`
The me` unseen-the groundless me`.

(George Walters-Sleyon)

Advancing the same assertion for the holistic nature of the person is the argument presented by Pope John Paul II. The pope presents a critique of the socially constructed notion of human beings and its distortion of what he calls the "culture of being."

Pope John Paul II

Suspicious of the twentieth century's materialistic understanding of the person, John Paul II contends that the dignity of the human being can only be established in relation to the image of God[137] that is present in every human being. The image of God is the only possible means of beholding individuals as human beings and not as creatures devoid of significance. For the pope, and St. Augustine, the African Bishop, the importance of the person in the eyes of God is reflected in the Incarnation: Jesus Christ taking on human flesh. He writes,

> In reality, it is only in the mystery of the Word made flesh that the mystery of man truly becomes clear . . . Christ the new Adam, in the very revelation of the mystery of the Father and of his love, fully reveals man to himself and brings to light his most high calling . . . Human nature, by the very fact that it was assumed, not absorbed, in him, has been raised in us also to a dignity beyond compare. For, by his incarnation, he, the Son of God, has in a certain way united himself with each man.[138]

---

[137]. Fr. Thomas McGovern, *The Christian Anthropology of John Paul 11*: An Overview www. Christendom-awake.org/pages/mcgovern/chrisanthro. htm 35.

[138]. Vatican Council 11, *Gaudium et Spes* (GS) (The Church in the Modern World, 1965) and *Dignitatis Humanae* (Decree on Religious Freedom, 1965). 22.

LOCKED UP AND LOCKED DOWN

As someone who experienced the carnage of war, its psychological impact and who also saw the impact of human cruelty to one another, the pope can only talk about "human flourishing" and what it means from the perspective of the incarnation of Jesus Christ. The incarnation is important because it uncovers the divine nature and destiny of the human being.[139] In Christ, man is truly revealed. The pope's assertion of persons as created in the image of God provides the basis for persons as living within a social environment with other persons who are created in the image of God. It is in this context that we can derive an adequate understanding of human beings and human development. The pope condemns assumptions and perceptions that breed inequalities, subjugation and war, hunger and malnourishment, illiteracy and oppression. His condemnation of the social crisis of the world reflects his rejection of the prevailing trend of economic disparities characteristic of our world today with the concentration of wealth in the hands of the few while the majority linger in poverty. It is also in this regard that we can fully grasp the link between poverty, marginalization, racism, illiteracy, alienation, injustice, crime, violence, social unrest, distrust, apathy and the high rates of detained and incarcerated black men. Pope John Paul II condemns the consumer-based notion of life that has emerged as contributing to the commodification and distortion of what he calls the "culture of being." Speaking in 1987 in Chile, Pope John Paul II asserted his call for the recognition of the true value of every human being. He writes,

> A process of reflection is necessary, which leads to a renewed diffusion and defense of the fundamental values of man as man, and in relation to other persons and to the natural surroundings in which he lives.[140]

---

[139]. An over view www. Christendom-awake.org/pages/mcgovern/ chrisanthro.htm.) Fr. McGovern, pg.

[140]. John Paul 11, "*The Task of the World Culture of Today Is to Promote the Civilization of Love*" (3 April 1987) no. 4, in English language weekly edition of L'Osservatore Romano (4 May 1987): 5

Finally, for Pope John Paul II, the person is a human being who is in "solidarity" with other persons with the goal of arriving at the "common good." In St. Augustine's argument for self-certainty, we see the rejection of the devaluation of the person to thinghood propagated by the prison-industrial complex.

Both St. Augustine and Pope John Paul II assert the claim for one's relationship to God as the source of human origin. It is the struggle for human dignity, the quest to establish the ontological ground for human dignity and the passion to assert the recognition for human dignity in the face of debilitating circumstances engendered by human activities. St. Augustine's process of deriving knowledge about self leads to self-certainty that is fundamentally introspective. He begins by looking within, for within one finds the grounds for self-certainty. This exercise for St. Augustine is primary to the understanding of self. True identity is based on self-certainty, and this self-certainty is first derived from within, from the immaterial to the material to fully ground the material, i.e., from the soul's relationship with God to the body to establish true self-identity. The existential angst of the more than one million black men in federal and county prisons and detention facilities cannot be adequately explained without an analysis of how people are perceived and categorized. As Muelder intimates, their sentence is as a result of the conviction of vengeful penology and financial gain. It is in this context that one can adequately understand the conviction and sentiments expressed in John Wesley's letter to William Wilberforce in Wilberforce's fight for the abolition of slavery and the slave trade. He writes,

> Dear Sir: Unless the divine power has raised you, us to be a *Athanasius contra mundum,* I see not how you can go through your glories enterprise in opposing that execrable villainy which is the scandal of religion, of England, and of human nature. Unless God has raised you up for this very thing, you will be worn out by the opposition of men and devils. But if God be for you, who can be against you? Are all of them together stronger than God? O be not weary of well doing! Go on, in the name of God and in the power of his might, till even American slavery (the vilest that ever saw the sun) shall vanish away before it. Reading this morning a tract written by a poor African, I was particularly struck by that

circumstances that a man who has a black skin, being wronged or outraged by a white man, can have no redress; it being a 'law' in our colonies that the *oath* of a black against a white goes for nothing. What villainy is this?[141]

Wesley wrote to encourage Wilberforce in the fight to end slavery because Wesley was a man of God. He knew that one who held the Scripture in high esteem need not be told that every mortal being has the spark of the divine in them and that every human being is created in the very image of God. For Wesley, adding his voice and prayers to the fight for the recognition of the divine foundation of every human being was comparable to nothing because he understood the shared mutuality of human interconnectedness. Wesley's support against slavery was based on the conviction that the essence of the slaves as human beings was not material and economical but immaterial.

In the search for the authentic person, in Augustine we find a cogent theological analysis of self and the quest for self-certainty that is fundamental to the black person's sense of personhood. But in Dr. W. E. B. Du Bois, we find the quest for answers to another question, questions regarding the racialized person.

> **I dwell in the Permanent**
> **For the Preeminent is within**
> **To dwell in the permissive**
> **Is to dwindle in perplexity**
> **Therefore I gasp at profundity**
> **And wither the paralysis**
>
> **(George Walters-Sleyon)**

W. E. B. Du Bois and the Racialized Person

Why is the person of African descent in America or the Diaspora interested in the questions of race? In *The Conservation of Races*, Du

---

[141.] *http://gbgm-umc.org/umw/Wesley/wilber.stm, Wesley's Thoughts on Slavery: http://docsouth.unc.edu/church/wesley/wesley.html, http://www. history.ucsb.edu/faculty/marcuse/classes/2c/texts/17, http://gbgm-umc. org/umw/wesley/thoughtsuponslavery.stm*

Bois asserts that the black person in America has always felt the need to discuss the "destinies and origins of races primarily because in the back of most discussions of race with which he is familiar, have lurked certain assumptions as to his natural abilities, as to his political, intellectual and moral status which he felt were wrong."[142] Du Bois defines race as a "social construction" influenced by environmental and social factors.

Du Bois was forever critical of the use of race for, the justification of evil perpetrated against blacks in the name of self-defense. He gave four reasons why race antagonism was used as a justification: first, a "repulsion" from something "evil" or "harmful" and therefore an instrument of survival, second, "a reasonable measure of self-defense against undesirable racial traits," third, "racial antipathy is a method of race development" and finally, race antipathy as a "method of group specialization" (Du Bois: *Does Race Antagonism Serve Any Good Purpose,* published in 1914 in *The Crisis*). Under these conditions, the Negro in America is often caught in a psychological malady in search of his or her true identity.

"Double consciousness" is the phrase coined by Du Bois to capture the "pain" of existential "blackness." It reflects an existential experience that tries to capture the sense of nothingness. Double consciousness implies an inner tension within one's self. The black person's selfhood is defined in reference to external factors that contradict their true sense of self. Double consciousness is a scrutinizing experience of self that question one's sense of self worth and humanity. It is the perception that the black person is an illusion, to be seen but not to be heard. Double consciousness is living behind the veil. According to Du Bois,

> the Negro is a sort of seventh son, born with a veil, and gifted with second-sight in this American world,-a world which yields him no true self-consciousness, but only lets him see himself through the revelation of the other world, it is a peculiar sensation, this double-consciousness, this sense of always

---

142.   Phil Zuckerman. The Social Theory of W.E.B. Du Bois, (London: Pine Forge Press, 2004) 19. Du Bois, W. E. B. *The Conservation of Races: Published in 1897 in the Occasional Papers of the America Negro Academy.*

LOCKED UP AND LOCKED DOWN

> looking at one's self through the eyes of others, of measuring one's soul by the type of a world that looks on in amused contempt and pity. One feels his two-ness—an American, a Negro; two souls, two thoughts, two unreconciled strivings; two warring ideals in one dark body, whose dogged strength alone keeps it from being torn asunder (Du Bois: *The Souls of Black Folk*, pg. 2).

Double consciousness is the dilemma faced by the black individual to be "white" when they are black, the contradiction of being a part yet an "other," of being an insider, yet an outsider or of knowing oneself to be a subject yet seen as an object, the anxiety to imitate white culture yet confined to black culture, the tension to be judged by white paradigms yet delighting in black pride, the frustration to be original yet considered a duplicate, the anguish of rejection yet seemingly accommodated. It is characterized as the experience of nothingness, limitation of self, an existential despair of coming to the end of one's options and alternatives, but only with the fear of doom and nothingness. Double consciousness captures the subtle agony of the black person as fractured by several social roles and identities which are often in tension with one another while struggling to remain certain of self. Those who have crossed this threshold through academic, social, and material advancement know what it means, yet are haunted by the scars of twoness. But Du Bois must articulate this hopelessness of self in the presence of pain; the threat of self by self. Self is presented as an opposition to itself instead of self-affirming itself, the threat of being by nonbeing in its brutal torture of the me in me, the I in me to the point of subtle agony. To experience double consciousness is to experience the pain of racism, racialization, commodification, racial profiling, thinghood, objectification and unjust detention, and incarceration. It is to be interpreted simply on the basis of one's blackness. To understand the magnitude of this experience is to delve into the subtle scrutiny and suspicion that confronts the dreams and aspirations of the black man. It is the suspicion associated with every transaction of the black entrepreneur, and that reduces to psychological blackness every achievement of the black intellectual, Du Bois, like the melancholic poet, must lament the meaninglessness of this experience. It is because the black person is asked to empty himself of his African heritage. He is asked to pour out of himself his blackness, he is asked to purify himself of his Negroness, he is asked to purify himself of himself, and since such a request entails the distortion of his sense of consciousness, Du Bois must bring into absurdity the meaninglessness of such a request and exclaim:

> What, after all, am I? Am I an American or am I a Negro? Can I be both? Or is it my duty to cease to be a Negro as soon as possible and be an American? If I strive as a Negro, am I not perpetuating the very cleft that threatens and separates Black and White America? Is not my only possible practical aim the seduction of all that is Negro in me to the American? Does my black blood place upon me any more obligations to assert my nationality than German, or Irish or Italian blood would? (Du Bois, *The Conservation of Race*).

For Du Bois, this is the source of his inner-dividedness since he is forced to continuously look within himself. Du Bois like Augustine must travel on an introspective path, one that involves the looking within. Both were great intellectuals of astute minds and intelligence, yet both must introspect to find the "Ground of their being," the root of being human, and the river of their being to assert self as self. For Augustine, it was a religious journey of conversion. Augustine was interested in knowing God as a result of which he could know himself. Du Bois' was a journey to understand self in light of his social debilitations. His journey was philosophical, existential, and spiritual. Du Bois must question his sense of being in an environment that saw the color of his skin for who he was, his black race as his own limitation. Only if he was white, he would be accepted. He must question his existence and ask for responses, and because responses could not readily be found, he must resort to the liberty of the pen, the typewriter, and the writing pad. Du Bois' search for answers and authentic self was not simply a rational philosophical inquiry to satisfy his rational ego. Du Bois' existential inquiry was to discover self and answers, which this existential location demanded. This existential search for self birthed in him the agony of unjust treatment faced by the black person on the street, in the ghettos, in the alleys, the cells, the prisons, the detention facilities, and the fields. Like them, he must become restless till he tells their story, articulate their anxieties, and capture their despair in words, with his soul, his heart, and his pen.

Du Bois came to understand the black experience as a collective experience. In attempting to articulate this inner demise, this splitting of oneself within, he saw racism as a problem that was becoming global, and devastating. He argued that it was a problem that blinded the eyes of its perpetrators, deafened the ears of those who champion it, and hardened the hearts of those it benefitted. The benefit, privilege, status, and power racism accrues must ceaselessly flow for generations to come while it afflicts the lives of its victim. He saw the life of the racist and the racialized as two painful lives characterized by the departure from integration to disintegration, from similarity to dissimilarity, from unity to disunity. Racism, tribalism, and other forms of exclusionary consciousness resist the need to recognize the idea of shared human connectedness and mutuality. The cord that holds humanity in oneness must be fractured, broken, and eventually abandoned. Du Bois must articulate this pain in the face of the racialization of self in opposition to self to avoid self-distortion. He cannot stand this duplicity and the cognitive dissonance of self toward self occurring within. He knows that tension often arises between those who recognize this shared mutuality between all human beings existing interdependently and those who refuse to recognize it and desire to perpetuate a distorted view of humanity for personal self-interest. Du Bois saw racism as a problem and could articulate it as fundamentally influencing and permeating sociopolitical and economic activities on a global scale. He writes,

> The problem of the twentieth century is the problem of the color-line-the relation of the darker to the lighter races of men in Asia and Africa, in America and the islands of the sea." (*Du Bois, The Souls of Black Folk pg. 9*).

Writing in the late nineteenth and twentieth century, Du Bois' painstaking social analysis investigated issues of power imbalances. For Du Bois, the "color line belts the world."[143] In his analysis, separation based on race is the determining factor in the formulation of sociopolitical, economic, and religious policies and practices. The color line determines black/white social relationships.

---

143. Eric Sundquist, *W. E. B Du Bois Reader.* (Oxford: Oxford University Press, 1994) 6.

One cannot dismiss the fact that Du Bois was a pioneer. Without a doubt, the gloomy picture of the late nineteenth and early twentieth centuries reflecting the demise of black people has been greatly altered. Blacks have been able to penetrate certain sociopolitical and economic structures that were mere dreams to Du Bois and others, though they were very optimistic about the intellectual capability of blacks. The United States has a black president in the person of Barack H. Obama today, a great accomplishment in light of the history of this country. Yet how do we explain the fact that black men constitute more than half of the detained and incarcerated population in the prisons of the United States at the dawn of the twenty-first century when the entire black population is only 12 to 13% of the entire population of the United States? This is the problem that the Church must begin to address as a body without reference to race, creed or color.

The above analysis is an attempt to understand the consciousness informing the criminalization of black men in America, the high rate of incarceration and detention of black men, and the disproportionality in relation to the effects of the commercial prison—industrial complex. It is an attempt to derive a way of speaking to a bewildered group of men whose sense of identity, destiny, and understanding is undermined by racial sentencing, criminalization, racial profiling, and the commercial enterprise of the prison-industrial complex.

It is difficult to change people's perception about who you are, especially if you are seen through the prism of race. But you can change yourself from within and view the outside from within instead of allowing the outside to dictate your sense of being and personhood. It is in this regard that I believe that the role of the Body of Christ in America, not only the Black Church and Missionary churches, is pivotal. The Black Church has historically served as a "city of refuge" for the community. The birth of the Black Church is characterized by the black experience of despair and anxiety in this social milieu, and it must be willing to do so again on a collective level. With the exception that this time, it is not only for black men as African Americans but also black men as African immigrants from Africa and the Caribbean lingering between indefinite detention and indefinite deportation.

Chapter Five

A Call to the Black Church

It is a great irony that the Negro church has figured so largely as a rallying center for the civil rights movement in the South primarily because of its strategic position as an institution in Negro life; it has not become a civil rights rallying center because of its religious ethical teaching as such. But the logic of the impact of the religious experience in the Negro church made it inevitable that it would become such a center. For a long time the Negro church was the one place by the white community. A man may be buffeted about by his environment, or may be regarded as a nobody in the general community; a woman may be a nurse in a white family in which the three-year-old child in her care calls her by her first name, thus showing quite unconsciously the contempt in which she is held by his parents. When this Negro man and this Negro woman come to their church, however, for one terribly fulfilling moment they are somebody. (Dr. Howard Thurman *With Head and Heart: The Autobiography of Howard Thurman*)

The Black Church has historically been the harbinger of the black religious experience. Its pivotal role as a place of refuge for the weary souls cannot be overstated. The Black Church has withstood social forces to construct its identity and reality. Whether it was socially imposed from above or social forces generated from within, the Black

Church has been able to meaningfully interpret its existence within the context of these forces. The Black Church has also engendered the construction of social forces that have shaped the social ethos of the American social milieu. In its intrinsic experience of God and the translation of the knowledge of that experience within the context of its social location, the Black Church has withstood its encroachment from outside. Through the shared experience of the transcendent presence of God in their midst, a synthesis of beliefs and practices used to construct meaning for individuals and collective initiatives has evolved to serve as a refuge for its troubled souls. For the Black Church, religious experience is ineffable, mental, social, transcendental, and phenomenological. The spiritual context is the engagement with God. The communal context is the Black Church and the context for the construction of meaning and interpretation of its social reality. It consists of the existential experiences and implications of slavery, segregation, racism, black-on-black crime, AIDS in the black community, the incarceration and detention of black men, concentrated poverty, triumphs, victory, failures, and successes. According to Dale Andrews, the "refuge" image of the Black Church is historically the interpretation of the existential role of the Black Church in the black community. While resisting what he refers to as "adversarial posturing and deafness"[144] on the part of those who criticize the Black Church as being only "other-worldly," Andrews contends that

> this image includes concerns for the survival, nurture, and growth of African Americans through the Christian faith. The church fulfilled the emotional, spiritual, and sociological needs of an alienated people. It provided a community that affirmed and nurtured black community, black humanity and worth in an otherwise hostile and degrading social existence. This safe space was not static. Community provided proactive space for personality development and human relations. The effect was empowerment for living anew.[145]

---

144. Dale Andrews, *Practical Theology For Black Churches: Bridging Black Theology and African American Folk Religion* (Louisville: Westminster John Knox Press, 2002) 9.

145. Ibid., 34.

LOCKED UP AND LOCKED DOWN

He goes on to contend that the refuge image was engendered as a "corporate identity"[146] fostered in the midst of slavery and discrimination for the benefit of "both human and spiritual bonding" and "human community and relatedness."[147] Andrews argues that the Black Church "has commonly fostered black wholeness and human rights."[148] As a "protective community" in the midst of discrimination and racism, the Black Church, against the criticism of being simply concerned with nonsocial activities, has done so by establishing a "sociopolitical presence" that came to be existentially developed as a space "for the critical affirmation of human value and human needs, which included liberation."[149] Accordingly, the Black Church is therefore caught in this moment of salvation and liberation, "spiritual faith and liberation,"[150] the cultivation of both "spiritual and social liberation"[151] for the holistic liberation of the black person. Andrews is convinced that "liberation can begin only in the black community"[152] through the Black Church translating the liberating message of the gospel of Jesus Christ into concrete actions.

Commenting on the origin of the Black Church, Emmanuel McCall argues that the despair and anguish of racism is the "birth pang of the black church."[153] It became a Black Church because of the experience of slavery, slaves, and ex-slaves attempting to make sense of their sociopolitical, social-cultural, and economic conditions. But not only were these experiences pivotal to the formation of what is now referred to as the Black Church, but the fact that slaves and ex-slaves could not be allowed to "worship God" together with their white masters. While various slaves and ex-slaves worship communities eventually took on the designation of their former masters' denominations, they transformed the borrowed practices to reflect their existential

---

146. Ibid., 35.

147. Ibid., 35.

148. Ibid., 35.

149. Ibid., 36.

150. Ibid., 36.

151. Ibid., 8.

152. Ibid., 36.

153. Charles Foster, *Black Religious Experience: Conversation on Double Consciousness and The work of Grant Shockley* (Nashville, Abingdon, 2003). 9

experience. It is in this regard that what is called the Black Church emerged. In describing the theological thrust of the Black Church, McCall surmises that "the practicing of religion for the black church is a theology of survival . . . I must underscore the fact that the black church is the carrier of black folk culture. If you want true authentic American black culture, you must go to the black church."[154] The Black Church was a source of social unity, serving as a sociocultural and educational center. The Black Church then, and in several ways today, provides communal wholeness. It serves as the center for social and spiritual activities. He writes, "When the world and the society in which we lived were constantly tearing us apart, the church continued to help us to get it together, to 'get it all together.'"[155]

The black religious experience is shaped by this "twoness" of their social reality. It implies existence on a dual plane of consciousness, both historically influenced and religiously influenced. The understanding of this "dual existence" is fundamental to understanding the development of the African American religious practice. This understanding existentially provides the religious and social contexts for the construction of meaning. But this socioreligious construction of reality does not simply take place in the "public sphere" but in the Black Church, which provides the context for individual and collective character and theological formation. Commenting on the pivotal role of the Black Church, Grant Shockley intimates that

> in their sermons, spirituals, prayers and Sunday school teachings, Black people came to terms with their blackness, their expressional gifts, and their social situation of slavery and brutalizing oppression in a white-racist church and society. There is where they "worked out their salvation" in relation to questions of their bondage, their separation from family, their chattel status, their idea of good and evil, of God and Satan. From its beginning in the time of slavery, the church came to have a particular significance to black people because it provided them with a "gathered community" of relative freedom, expressional outlet, community information, group

---

[154.] Foster, *Black Religious Experience.*, 13

[155.] Ibid., 14.

solidarity, personal affirmation, mutual aid, and leadership development.[156]

The church became a meeting place, an opportunity for the creation of social ideas and meaning, the construction of identity and selfhood, the impetus for social relevance and action. The Black Church became a "second community" for African Americans living in the twilight of despair characterized by the search for "somebodiness." This "twoness" is understood as life in the nonchurch community and the church community, negation of selfhood and acceptance, in the Black Church where one is, is affirmed and in the nonchurch community where one is, and is "not." This twoness characterizes the Black religious experience. It is this process of becoming, of pursuing selfhood and personhood, both on the individual and collective level in the sociopolitical and economic worlds that meaning is constructed for the black man or woman. The Black Church is that place where meaningful construction took place. Individuals could forge a sense of identity. It is done based on the secured spaced provided from the storms raging on the outside, the bewilderment, the estrangement and the conflict with self experienced individually and collectively. To adopt Dr. Cornel West's existential definition of "nihilism" is vital in this context. Moving beyond the detached philosophical understanding of nihilism, West defines nihilism as "the lived experience of coping with a life of horrifying meaninglessness, hopelessness, and (most important) lovelessness."[157] As an age-old problem for blacks in America, nihilism reflects the threat to being, selfhood, the me of me by the absurd, by nonbeing. But West is very particular about the role of the Black Church as fundamental in standing as a buffer against raging storms from the outside especially for our contemporary time. He writes,

> The genius of our black foremothers and forefathers was to create powerful buffers to ward off the nihilistic threat, to equip black folk with cultural armor to bear back the demons of hopelessness, meaninglessness, and lovelessness. These buffers consisted of cultural structures of meaning and

---

[156]   Ibid., 32.

[157]   Cornel West, *Race Matters* (New York: Vintage Books, 2001), 22-23

feeling that created and sustained communities; this armor constituted ways of life and struggle that embodied values of service and sacrifice, love and care, discipline and excellence. In other words, traditions for blacks surviving and thriving under usually adverse New World conditions were major barriers against the nihilistic threat.[158]

Yet West laments the fact that things are not like the way they have been and blurts out the inevitable question, "What has changed? What went wrong?"[159]

These are some of the most pivotal questions that the Black Church through its preachers, pastors, deacons and deaconesses, and eventually its members should ponder as we seek for solutions to the predicament of the over one million detained and incarcerated black men in America today. While West in his search for answers makes a cogent argument for "the saturation of market forces and market moralities in black life and the present crisis in black leadership,"[160] can one claim that a level of insensitivity and apathy has emerged as a major obstacle in the black community? It is as though we have "arrived" on our own and whoever comes after us must struggle on his or her own. The result is indifference and detachment to one another's plight.

The number one social problem of the 21st century for the Black Church is the high rate of incarceration and detention of black men and especially it's health implications of HIV and AIDS. It is in this regards that West's assertion of the creation of "cultural structures" to ward off nihilism is relevant. How can the Body of Christ, specifically the Black Church and Missionary churches respond to this concern? Yes, black men have been disproportionately incarcerated in time past. The difference with this era of incarceration is that many black men are coming out of jails and prisons infected with HIV and AIDS, a cause for the high rate of HIV and AIDS in the black community. According to Marshall and the Human Rights Watch report, there are good reasons to believe that there are substantial links between the high rate of detained and incarcerated black men and the AIDS

[158.]   Ibid., 24

[159.]   Ibid., *Race Matters.*, 24

[160.]   Ibid., 24

epidemic in the black community. Sex between men and male rape in prisons is higher than female rape statistics. Consensual sex and non consensual sex as a result of rape takes place in prison without condoms. If human redemption is the thrust of the gospel as provided by the life, death, and resurrection of Jesus Christ, the Church should then ask itself what is the meaning of this claim of the gospel for our lives today? How can an adequate translation of the gospel of Jesus Christ that speaks to the existential condition and experience of incarcerated and detained black men be made?

The mission of the Church is to reach out to the world with the gospel of Jesus Christ—the evangelistic task of the Church, which is embedded within the mission of the Church, is to share the gospel. The objective of any evangelistic endeavor is to quicken the hearts of the people to a personal relationship with Jesus Christ. But this evangelistic responsibility does not negate the aspect of the Church's social responsibility. In fact, they are in several ways compatible. This compatibility in a very special way has always provided the foundation upon which the Church has existed.

According to Ben Johnson in his book *Rethinking Evangelism: A Theological Approach*, "The means for accomplishing the church's mission include the advocacy of policies . . . the exposure of unjust social structures, as well as the witness of individual members. The evangelistic means are proclamation, witness, fellowship, and personal invitation to faith in Christ. This personal witness takes place within the context of the church's larger mission."[161] The Church as a fellowship-community (Acts 2:43-47; 1 Cor. 14:23-25) creates an atmosphere for the process of conversion, transformation, and reformation of lives by its ability to give rise to structures for personal development and advancement. This idea does not legislate which comes first, conversion or social transformation. What is of utmost importance is the Church's willingness to intentionally establish structures in its ministry that will holistically cater to the spiritual and social concerns of its members. The undue emphasis on either one of these concerns will eventually lead to a nonholistic attitude without the requisite skills to foster the kind of spiritual and social development necessary for the lives of

---

161. Ben Johnson *Rethinking Evangelism: A Theological Approach* (Philadelphia: The Westminister Press, 1987) 79.

those in need. The goal is to intentionally develop social and spiritual relationships that foster a healthy communal life in the Church with influences on individual social and spiritual development. Evangelism of this nature is accompanied by intentional actions and deeds that compliment its activities. Its saves the evangelistic thrust of the church from slipping into a dysfunctional mode. A dysfunction evangelistic activity does not bring long-lasting results.

Andrews argues that the "care for others" must be primary to the "care for selves."[162] He contends that the growth of membership in churches in our day and time does not tally with the awareness of social concerns reflected by the growing social demands that intentionally seek the need for change. While most churches declare their intention for starting a "social ministry," their definition of social ministry often borders on internal concerns rather than external social concerns that affect the needs of the entire community. Andrews blames this kind of communal apathy on the permeation and centralization of American individualism in the Black Church's religious existence and, as a practical theologian, sees the solution in what he calls "prophetic preaching." He writes,

> In this cultural milieu, black churches have lost the covenant relation between spiritual intimacy with God and human care for others. American individualism disrupts God's will for humanity as revealed in the prophetic inspiration of a covenant community. Personal salvation is not the goal of redemption history; it is a 'beginning again.' Prophetic preaching not only insists upon human care but also maintains the correlation between human reflexivity and theological relationality, which characterizes prophetic consciousness. Prophetic ministry unites worship and praxis, salvation and social justice.[163]

The present predicament of increasing incarceration and detention of black men in America calls for the cultivation of ministries that are intentional to provide realistic solutions and answers. While the

---

[162.] Andrews, 130

[163.] Ibid., 130

influence of the Black Church in the lives of the present generation may not be as it was in the '50s or the '60s, Black and Missionary churches should be intentional in reaching out to black men. It means implementing structures that are biblically centered yet socially relevant. Missionary churches are those churches especially established by recent immigrants, and in this context from Africa and the Caribbean. These churches should intentionally cultivate members that are both socially and spiritually informed who will see the need to replicate such holistic understanding of the gospel of Jesus Christ in the black community. In this regard, the idea that we are our brother's keepers cannot be over emphasized. It is in this context that I present the next chapter as a search for tangible, realistic and workable solutions to the "Situation."

Chapter Six

What Do We Do?

To crush underfoot all prisoners in the land, to deny a man his rights before the Most High, to deprive a man of justice-would not the Lord see such things?
—Lamentations 3:34-36

Anyone who devotes himself to human duty according to the Christian formula, though outwardly he may seem to be immersed in the concerns of the earth, is in fact, down to the depths of his being, a man of great detachment.
—Pierre Teilhard De Chardin, *The Divine Milieu*

While the just detention and incarceration as a result of a crime committed is appropriate, the situation of arbitrary arrest, racially motivated sentencing influenced by the criminalization of black men, disproportional rate of detention and incarceration of black men and their commodification by the commercial prison—industrial complex is problematic. Apart from other consequences, it is problematic because of its immediate socioeconomic and health implications. We should all be concerned. It is not a black or white issue; it is one that should convict the conscience of humanity. The over one million black men and youths detained and incarcerated need the attention of all who have recognized the shared mutuality of human connectedness regardless of race, creed, or color. Jesus Christ said, "Whatever you did for one of the least of these brothers of mine, you did for me."[164]

Below are four responses: prophetic response, rational response, critical response, and pragmatic response developed for prescriptive reasons. They are not exhaustive neither do they purport to be absolute. They are responses developed as a result of my research. I am convinced that what I saw during my five days of detention at the federal detention facility is a symptom of a frightening picture for over one million black men in the prison system across the United States. These responses are constructed with the understanding that they will be used as a frame of reference by churches and organizations to initiate programs relevant to the situation of the detained, incarcerated, and commodified black men in the commercial prison—industrial complex.

A Prophetic Response

A prophetic response asserts the claim for the recognition of the inherent right of all human beings. As human beings like all human beings, black people have an inherent sense of dignity and worth that transcends color and racial particularities. To reduce the black man simply to color and to execute justice in this regard is to embark upon a process of ontological distortion. Based on the prevailing evidence, the proclivity to consider race and racial factors in the arrest and sentencing process ultimately results to a form of psychological distortion. Because this distortion is first ontological, affecting the being of the black person, it fundamentally distorts their self-image. It perpetuates the criminalization of black persons in the eyes of others, thus institutionalizing a stereotypical view of black people. The consequences are enormous, affecting the black family structure, the raising and rearing of children, black marriages, etc.

Ontological distortion affects the individual's sense of being, their sense of humanness and personhood. It manifests itself in forms of hopelessness, despair, black-on-black crime, and psychological struggle for survival. A healthy and assured sense of personhood should

---

[164.] Matt. 25: 40

fundamentally buttress an individual's sense of existence. The black person is often confronted by their own existential sense of being and personhood in a conflicting way. The criminalization of the black man is one of the greatest fears of the professional black man. Regardless of his qualification and personal development, he and his works are often subjected to criminalizing and suspicious scrutiny that subjects him to depersonalizing tendencies. He must strive to excel but is often caught in this dilemma of not doing his best because his best is scrutinized through the prism of racial lenses. The professional who is black may have had a good family upbringing with positive role models and a secured and protective home. His experience may be different from the black man who grew up in the projects or ghetto and is struggling to make it through his education with a dysfunctional family background. He is faced with the possibility of dropping out of school, internalizing what society says about him, and eventually becoming a part of the prison statistics. This is not to forget the option that standing up to these challenges, knowing that sometimes he will never be given an A in school no matter how good his work might be, will pay off in the future. Yet how difficult the struggle is, knowing that your best work is often scrutinized through racial lenses and you must constantly settle for B or B+, never getting the A+ or A that the instructor knows you deserve.

It becomes even more difficult when a structural and institutional argument is made for the justification of such an ontological distortion. With more black men seemingly in jail than in college, with more black men disproportionally detained and incarcerated because of racial particularities, with more black men receiving three strikes sentences, with more black men lacking employment skills and receiving poor quality education in public schools, with more black neighborhoods substantially declining into abject poverty, with increased fatherlessness because of the disproportionality in detention and incarceration rate of black men, with more single mothers raising boys and girls while stressed out, and working two or three jobs, etc., the prognosis for the community is unsettling. Where are the men of productive age to further perpetuate the community? Where are the men of sound mental faculty to handle community affairs? Do we understand the twenty to thirty years impact of this disproportionate incarceration of black men? It is difficult not to describe this as an intentional or intentionally subconscious expression of historical insensitivity and intolerance.

The equality and dignity accorded all human beings is first defined as a divine awareness based on the spark of God in every human being. The immaterial nature of the person transcends race and racial features, political and social constructs, economic worth and religious affiliation. Racial disparity as an intentional and unintentional construct in the administration of justice negates the very essence of justice. A justice system that has a proclivity to subject justice to racial particularities inversely undermines its own praxis. While the immediate negative impact of a race-centered justice system may be positively felt by the group or individuals for whom it is executed and negatively against whom it is executed, it undermines the principles and structures of justice. It is this notion of justice that Jesus condemned as the worst expression of human insensitivity and intolerance in human social relations.

In Luke 18: 1-8, Jesus enjoins his disciples to embark upon a life of prayer in view of his imminent crucifixion and ultimate return. Between these two events, he sought to present in the form of a parable as he always did, a picture of human social relations and practices in the world. The judge is presented as a type of legislator formulating and executing rules for adequate social engagement and community development.

Between the judge and God is the pathetic widow who is culturally susceptible to social biases and impartiality because of her gender and widowhood. She is perhaps on the verge of losing her land or home left to her by her dead husband either to his family, or her son is about to be taken into slavery by a debtor, or she is about to be thrown on the streets to become a beggar because of a false accusation. She is weak, desolate, defenseless, and helpless with no powerful friends to appeal to. Her only means of intervention and remedy is the available justice system. Jesus presents her as the reason for justice. Her poor condition does not necessitate justice but demands the execution of justice as the necessary means for handling her case. Yet the response of the judge in this case is not assuring.

The judge does not "fear God," he does not "care for men," "neither regard men." He is simply afraid that the widow's persistence will ruin him: "So she won't eventually wear me out with her coming" (verse 4-5, NIV) he says to himself, therefore he will get justice for her. In contrast to this judge, God as a judge is presented as ready to execute justice for those who cry in their anxiety and destitution to him. While the judge as the sociopolitical custodian of justice is refraining from executing justice for the widow in her desolation, God, on the other hand, is seen as moving quickly to implement justice. The judge will only execute justice for the widow because it will keep her from bothering him. Furthermore, to intervene on the widow's behalf might enhance his image as a judge and secure his status, secure his personal and family comfort, enhance his reputation for possible advancement in the judicial structure or national politics as he contemplates running for public office. He is terribly indifferent, and Jesus calls him an "unjust judge."

Most important to Jesus are the other two expressions of the judge: he does not fear God, and he has no regard for men/humanity. Because he does not fear God, he does not recognize that justice is divine. Because he does not recognize that justice is divine, he cannot objectively execute justice as the inherent right of the "most disadvantaged." For him, justice as "free and equal" for every human being for whom the "fair-terms" of justice at most seeks to "satisfy" in the society is qualified.[165] He relies upon the sociopolitical construction of justice that is historically constructed and influenced by human understanding, assumptions, and self-interest. He does not want to know or does not want to acknowledge that justice is divine.

Jesus is expressing the fact that injustice is painful because justice is divine. As divine, justice is symbolic of the nature of God. In several places in the Old Testament, God is presented as the God of justice, a just and righteous judge, and as justice personified. Justice is first divine because it has an ontological foundation. The judge does not understand this nature of justice since he does not fear God. He resists justice as divine because an ontological understanding of justice easily convicts his sense of consciousness and seeks to reshape his socially constructed sense of justice. This socially constructed sense of justice provides eyes, feet, and hands for justice. In contrast, justice as divine is blind, impartial, pure, and transcending the narrowness of human assumptions. For this judge, justice as the spirit of social harmony is distorted, justice as the harbinger of creative unity is defiled, justice as the ethos of human compatibility

---

165. John Rawls, *Justice as Fairness: A Restatement* (New Delhi, Universal, Low Publishing Co. Pvt. Ltd. 2001).

is destroyed. Justice as the sublime in human relationship is discarded and made secondary for material and sensual reasons.[166]

The judge does not fear God, and secondly he does not regard men nor care for men. His rejection of an ontological basis for justice leads to narcissistic and solipsistic definition and execution of justice. Because of his self-interest and apathetic view of justice, justice is executed as a misanthrope would. He does not care or regard other human beings. As a narcissist, he takes pride in his accomplishment and disregards the accomplishment of others, symbolic of the beautiful youth who is enamored by his beauty; he craves himself and his comfort. As a solipsist, he exists for himself and nothing else. His experience and social location alone provides the paradigm for life. What a pathetic experience to stand in front of a judge who hates God, hates other human beings, is in love with himself and him alone, and does not understand or desire to understand the experience and pain of others except his own. He carries the view that "only I exist." Everything external to me depends upon my existence. The existence of the external world is secondary. He portrays the traits of a typical solipsist: "Only my pain is real." The solipsist claims his or her experience is the only "real" experience. "When anything is seen, it is always I who sees it."[167] Only the person who has such an experience can claim that experience. It leads to social confusion because all other experiences must be defined and validated by the solipsist's single experience.

According to Jesus, the danger is reflected in the intolerance and insensitivity exhibited toward the widow. Her plight does not affect him, except her physical presence, which is a nuisance to him. What about her pain, her tears, and the agony she must bear because of her social, political, and economic situation and the fact that if he does not intervene expeditiously, she might end up on the street as a beggar or something worst? He refuses to recognize the fact that she is a widow in a society that regards widows as burdens to the deceased husband's family. Jesus calls him an "unjust" judge. He is a judge, but he is an unjust judge. He is unjust because he sits in the capacity of justice but executes injustice. For Jesus, it was more than going out to

---

[166]. Ibid.,

[167]. Ludwig Wittgenstein, *Blue and Brown Books* (USA, Harper and Row Publishers, 1958) PP. 57, 61, 63, 64.

intervene because of the pestilential activity of the widow. It was the totality of the heart's response to the pain, tears, and distress that his lack of objective justice reflects. Any form of justice that suffers from partiality, prejudice, and distortion to the level of disregarding the humanity of a person in Jesus's view is worst than no justice.

The painfulness of injustice is difficult to fathom and cannot go unchecked because the human being is created in the very image of God. The image of God implies the presence of the spark of God in every human person. That is why injustice cannot be tolerated for long. Justice must overthrow injustice because justice is divine, and injustice is ungodly. Injustice negates the ontological being of any person; it seeks to destroy the inherent dignity of a person and reduces them to material and corporeal objects; objects that can be commodified, used, abused, misused, and eventually discarded.

Injustice is painful because justice is divine. As ontological beings, human beings existentially feel the pain of injustice because of the spark of God within every human being. That is why the most uneducated and illiterate man or woman knows what is just and can identify justice and injustice. The spirit of justice is intuitively known and the spirit of injustice is also intuitively known because justice is innate. In this context, injustice is mainly as a result of cognitive dissonance: knowing the right thing to do for the other person but refusing to do it because of personal or social reasons. It does not only take education and intellectual sophistication to recognize injustice; it takes the spark of God, the "breath of God," and the image of God that defines the essential nature of every man and woman.

Jesus begins the parable with the call to pray and ends the parable with the need to have faith in prayer. I call this kind of praying proactive praying. Proactive praying in this context is the desire to see tangible transformation in the sociopolitical, economic, and religious life of the arbitrarily arrested, detained, and incarcerated black men in the criminal justice system. Proactive prayer is praying to see holistic transformation taking place in the lives of those detained and incarcerated that will lead to decline in the high rate of recidivism among black men and youths. Proactive praying in this regard is a means to achieve objective and impartial justice in three forms of engagement:

Firstly, proactive prayer is transformative engagement. It seeks transformation by engaging the sociopolitical and economic structures in a cogent manner that leads to change and decline in the arbitrary arrest, detention, and incarceration of black men. Proactive prayer as transformative engagement compels the Church to advance the claim for investigation in the three strike policy. As the various reports have shown, three strikes perpetually targets black youths and sentence them to 25 years in jail. Proactive prayer compels the Church to pursue investigation into the policies and practices defining the war on drugs because of the social and economic implications for the black family structures. As the studies by the Sentencing Project indicate, the use of drugs by blacks and its presence in the black community is far less prevalent as the media will have us to believe. While the consequences of drugs in the black community are devastating as a result of grave economic conditions, the Church should see the over one million detained and incarcerated black men as a serious symptom of arrest and incarceration influenced by the war on drugs with serious repercussion for black men, black youths and the black family. Proactive prayer as transformative engagement compels the Church to pursue knowledge and be aware of the activities of the commercial prison—industrial complex. The economic emphasis of the commercial prison—industrial complex is having a social impact that is destructive to the black family structure, a psychological impact that is debilitating; an economic impact that leads to generational impoverishment and economic marginalization, and health consequences of HIV and AIDS that are devastating.

Secondly, proactive prayer is transcendent engagement. Praying with this recognition appeals to God as the source for true and impartial justice for all. It argues for the recognition of the inherent dignity of all persons in the sentencing person. The prophetic response in this context makes the appeal for reform in the sentencing process based on the claims of the impact of ontological distortion and the commodification of black men by the prison-industrial complex.

Finally, proactive prayer is transparent engagement. Transparent engagement comes against the practice of cognitive dissonance reflected in the attitude of Christians and church leaders with respect to the prevailing situation. Transparent engagement convicts us and calls us to a life that seeks to bring into being the mind of God concerning every human being as we seek the face of God. This is not to dismiss the fact there are those who intentionally commit crimes worthy of the punishment they are receiving. But how can we account for over a million black men in detention, incarceration, and prison, over half of the total prison population in the United States, when the prevailing statistic points to causes of arrest and incarceration that are racially motivated? Transparent engagement convicts our refusal to address the issue of arbitrary arrest, detention, and incarceration of black men induced by lies, skin color, criminalization, and business rather than justice. For example, most suburbs will not have blacks purchase homes or rent in their communities. They can however, have blacks when they are "caged" as Marshall argues, in multimillion-dollar prison complexes located in the hearts of wealthy suburbs because of the economic benefits and tax breaks that comes along with the presence of these complexes. For Jesus, justice is divine. Justice as divine pushes us to the edge to look within, ask the hard questions, and embark upon the difficult actions. To implement justice is to execute a divine mandate for the common good and flourishing of humanity.

> *But the people that do know their God shall be strong, and do exploits . . . God is our refuge and strength, an ever present help in times of trouble. Therefore we will not fear.*
> —Daniel 11:32; Psalm 46: 1-2

A Rational Response

> *"The U.S Department of Justice estimates that 16% of the adult inmates in American prisons and jails—which means more than 350,000 of those locked up—suffer from mental illness, and the percentage in juvenile custody is even higher. Our correctional institutions are also heavily populated by the 'criminally ill,' including inmates who suffer from HIV/AIDS, tuberculosis, and hepatitis."*

> Senator Jim Web, *What's Wrong With Our Prisons?*
> *Boston Sunday Globe Parade, pp.4-5*

A rational response is a social response that is biblically informed. A rational response is not a philosophical and political treaty against unjust forms of detention and incarceration but a response that relates to the concrete experiences of arbitrary arrest, detention, and incarceration. The eighteenth century prison reform in England was started by Christian leaders who were appalled by the filth and diseased-ridden environment of prisons. While these particular situations may not relate to the disproportion evident in the detention and

LOCKED UP AND LOCKED DOWN

incarceration of black men in the twenty-first century, the sentiments expressed and the Christian debate crafted in favor of human dignity by John Wesley and others are worth emulating.

John Wesley started a prison ministry in 1730 as a part of his Oxford Methodists ministry. The concept of Wesley's ministry was built on his understanding of the teaching of Jesus in Matthew 25: 31-46. It was a ministry directed to help the poor and disadvantaged in the society. It included visitation, together with the sharing of the gospel message with the hope that transformation will take place in the heart of the prisoners. Prisons in this era were terribly dirty, dingy, and unsanitary. Prisoners were surviving on small meals and the lack of medical attention. Prison conditions were often unfavorable. Most of the diseases were contagious. Sarah Peters, a ministry colleague of Wesley, contacted what was called "jail fever" and died.

According to *Wesley's Journal,* he preached to forty-seven prisoners on death row at Newgate on December 26, 1784. Ludgage and Newgate prisons in London were found to be in terrible shape and were condemned by Wesley. Wesley was introduced to the prisons by one Mr. William Morgan. He writes,

> In the summer following Mr. M[organ] told me he had called at the goal to see a man that was condemned for killing his wife, and that from the talk he had with one of his debtors he verily believed that it would do much good if anyone would be at the pains now and then of speaking with them. This he so frequently repeated that on the 24th of August, 1730, my brother and I walked down with him to the Castle. We were so well satisfied with our conversation there that we agreed to go thither once or twice a week.[168]

These visits marked the beginning of Wesley's prison ministry as final ecclesiastical approval came from the bishop of Oxford's chaplain, Mr. Gerard. With his foundational text, Matt. 25: 31-46, Wesley and his colleagues were able to solicit funding for the ministry. Though it was

---

[168]. John Wesley: *The Works of John Wesley,* Eds. Richard Heitzenrater, W. Reginald Ward, The Bicentennial Edition, Vol. 19 (Nashville, Tennessee: Abingdon Press, 1990), 25: 337.

a bit difficult, the Oxford Methodists as they later called themselves were eventually able to get the ministry off the ground and running. But they had to get approval from every town through the advice of one Rev. Joseph Hoole, the vicar of Haxey.[169] Recorded in his diary on Monday, October 15, Wesley expanded his ministry activities to a prison that held French prisoners at Knowle. He writes,

> I walked up to Knowle, a mile from Bristol, to see the French prisoners. About eleven hundred of them, we were informed, were confirmed in that little place without anything to lie on but a little dirty straw, or anything to cover them but a few foul thin rags, either by day or night, so that they died like rotten sheep. I was much affected, and preached in the evening on Exodus 23: 9—'Thou shall not oppress a stranger; for ye know the heart of a stranger, seeing ye were strangers in the land of Egypt. Eighteen pounds were contributed immediately, which were made up [to] four and twenty the next day. With this we bought linen and woolen cloth, which were made up into shirts, waistcoats, and breeches.[170]

For Wesley, immigrants in prisons were no different from citizens in prisons; both groups were exposed to the same treatment. Not only was he concerned about clothing and feeding prisoners, Wesley was equally concerned about their education. On August 1, 1732, Wesley got a letter from a fellow Oxford Methodist about the reading ability of two prisoners.[171] But not everyone approved of Wesley's prison ministry. Opposition came from others who thought his work was an infringement and a nuisance. The oppositions were simply based on theological and denominational grounds. It seems the Methodists were

---

[169] Ibid., 25:341-342

[170] Ibid., 21:285

[171] Richard P. Heitzenrater, *The Bicentennial Edition,* vol. 21 (Nashville, Tennessee: Abingdon Press, 1992,) 25: 331-334. "Two of the felons likewise have paid their fees and gone out, both of them able to read might well. John Clanville, who reads but moderately, and the horse-dealer, who cannot read at all. He knows all his letters and can spell most of the common monosyllables. I hear them both read three times a week . . ."

gaining more footholds in the prisons, and the Church of England did not look on this kind of activity favorably.

Wesley's prison activities, like his ardent condemnation of slavery and the Trans Atlantic Slave Trade, emerged as a result of his salvation experience and the fact that the gospel of Jesus was holistic in its appeal to human estrangement from God and self. It was experiences like these that helped Wesley to formulate his holistic understanding of the gospel of Jesus into what he called "scriptural holiness" and "social holiness."

Both scriptural holiness and social holiness underscore the understanding that salvation and renewal in Christ Jesus were the fundamental inspiration for social action. While social actions have their positive influences, they have the tendency to be strictly secularized. The limitation of a secularized-based social action in this context is its lack of emphasis on conversion and transformation. Wesley believed that scriptural holiness informs social holiness in its social activities, and it was a fundamental responsibility for every Methodist and expectation of every Christian to recognize this holistic understanding of the gospel of Jesus Christ. For Wesley, an emphasis on scriptural holiness without a participation in social holiness or vice versa was an incomplete Christian experience. He believed a transformed individual must work toward the transformation of his or her community and environment.[172]

For Wesley, social holiness was not limited to individual actions for transformation. He believed that transformation had to be structural, and those structural changes had to take place also in the corridors of the governing sociopolitical and economic systems. This conviction in Wesley was evident in his concern for prison reform and the criminal justice system. He was particularly convinced that the criminal justice system of England at the time needed to open its eyes to the horrible condition in which the prisoners were held and the dehumanizing consequences they must endure as a result of their imprisonment. Wesley saw this inhumane treatment of those imprisoned as a reproach on England as a Christian nation to the extent to which he could vent his frustration against the English legal system: "O England, England! Will this reproach never be rolled away from thee? Is there anything like this to be found either among Papists, Turks, or heathens? In the name of truth, justice, mercy,

---

[172]   Ronald Stone, *John Wesley's Life & Ethics* (Nashville, Abingdon Press 2001).

and common sense, I ask . . ."[173] Wesley eventually made prison visitation mandatory for all Methodist preachers. He was convinced that he had received a mandate from God to address the condition of prisons and prisoners. As a result, all who came into his fellowship had to likewise follow this mandate of God.[174] Wesley was affected by the shared sense of human mutuality regardless of race, class, education, nationality, etc. It is in this regard that I feel the Black Church and the entire Body of Christ can collaborate to pursue changes in the sentencing process and reform in the activities of the commercial prison—industrial complex

In view of the above, a rational response makes the claim for a second chance. Based on the prevailing statistics, a rational appeal calls for the reformulation of sentencing policies, police policies, and practices that arbitrarily single out black men as illegal for deportation and as criminals for incarceration, thus putting their families into grave financial, social, and psychological difficulties. It must be stated explicitly that my critique is not to eliminate punishment for criminals

---

[173.] In Donald Henry Kirkham's "*Pamphlet Opposition to the Rise of Methodism: The Eighteenth-Century English Evangelical Revival Under Attack,*" (PhD, diss., Duke University, 1973, p. 202) 21: 333

[174.] According to Rev. Brad Thie Rev. "From the beginning, ministry to prisoners was part of the established repertoire of Methodist activity. In 1778 it was confirmed by a Conference decision and made obligatory for all preachers.",—"Wesley's prison ministry belies his being 'tenacious of every point relating to decency.' He continuously ministered despite opposition from theological opponents, irritation form turnkeys, and the threat of serious disease and death. He courageously entered the penal system at a time when it was not fashionable to do so either theologically or socially. He did so consistently, and upheld the vitality of prison ministry in the Rules of the United Societies and in 'The Character of a Methodist.' Whether we label his social ethics a virtue or obligation ethic, or both, Wesley consistently nurtured this vital ministry that his friend William Morgan introduced him to in the summer of 1730. The prison ministry, for Wesley, was a critical focus for those who called themselves Methodists, lay and clergy alike. To continue to minister, and to be ministered to in prison settings, is an action congruent with reclaiming the rich heritage given to us by those who first called themselves Methodists." Brad Thie-WNCc-Revised 9/99 (*http://gbgm-umc. org/mission_programs/mcr/4.35/theprison.cfm*)

or to open the borders so that illegal aliens can flood the United States but to critique the racial consciousness and assumption influencing and informing the disproportion evident in the high rate of detention and incarceration of the black men as statistically evident and analyzed by several organizations. The Church's rational appeal is a humanitarian appeal inspired by the teachings of Jesus Christ in light of the negative consequences of the war on drugs and three strikes policies on the black community.

Another consequence of the disproportion evident in the high rate of detention and incarceration of black men is the link between the massive incarceration and detention of black men and the spread of HIV and AIDS, especially in the black community. One can surmise that the majority of those detained and incarcerated are heterosexuals, but as a result of the sexual culture of prisons and jails, many of them upon their release come out infected with HIV and AIDS. According to Melissa Santos writing in the Seattle Post-Intelligencer: "Members of the U.S. inmate population are nearly five times more likely to be infected with HIV than members of the general population" (*http://seattlepi.nwsource.com/local/300173_prison18. html.*) Others have argued that the "prevalence of HIV infection in U.S. prisons and jails is 6 to 10 times higher than that seen in the general free population . . . One study in 2002 estimated that about one-quarter of the U.S population infected with HIV had spent some time each year in a prison or jail. Hence, a certain number of prisoners who go in HIV negative come out HIV positive. Health experts say distributing condoms to these prisoners would be a wise approach to the problem" (*Free Condoms for Prisoners?*, *http://abcnews.go.com/print?id=* 2724605). Sexual activities do take place in prisons and jails and many of those sexual activities between male inmates are done without condoms:

> High risk behavior, particularly homosexual activity (consensual and non-consensual) is a given in the prison setting, and no correctional approach can eliminate it. Homosexual rape is commonplace as Justice Blackmun has observed, 'a youthful inmate can expect to be subjected to homosexual gang rape his first night in jail, or it has been said, on his way to jail. Weaker inmates become the property of stronger prisoners or gangs who sell the sexual service of the victim. United States v. Bailey 444 US 394 (*http://beyond-the-illusion.com/files/issues/condom.txt.*)

With more than one million black men detained and incarcerated, and black youths in juvenile facilities, the possibility of a continuous spread of HIV and AIDS in the black community cannot be denied. Consensual and nonconsensual sex between male inmates as a major health issue and the high rate of detention and incarceration of black men in the prison-industrial complex necessitate the Church's attention. The Church in America should be appalled by the spread of HIV and AIDS as a direct result of the over 2.4million people detained and incarcerated in the US prison system. An immediate solution is for the Church to advocate for the distribution of condoms to prisoners as part of the "comprehensive AIDS protection package." To advocate for the use of condoms may seem to encourage sex between inmates, however, the need to quell the spread of HIV and AIDS in the black community as a direct result of incarceration and detention cannot be easily dismissed. According to Eli Coleman, professor and director of the Program in Human Sexuality at the University of Minnesota Medical School, "whether legal or not, sex between inmates is occurring, and we must do what we can to provide vehicles for responsible sexual behavior, including the use of condoms" (*http://abcnews.go.com/print?id=2724605*). It is time the Church, especially the Black and Missionary churches take a proactive position and advocate for change in the policies affecting the more than one million detained and incarcerated black men. The long-term consequences could include a high proportion of black men with HIV and AIDS, decline of eligible black men for marriage, gradual breakdown of the family structure, more babies born with AIDS and increase in single parenting and fatherlessness. The Church can no longer afford to be silent. God is calling upon the Church to intervene for these men and stop the perpetual cycle of incarceration, HIV and AIDS infection, and recidivism.

A Critical Response

A critical response calls upon the black community to critique itself, to look in the mirror and put its house in order. A critical response demands that we assume responsibilities for those things we have done, measures we have failed to take that have contributed to the present demise. While we all agree that there are overshadowing historical and sociopolitical factors responsible for the mass incarceration and detention of black men, we must also acknowledge the fact that there are individual factors enhancing this mass incarceration.

As a result of American individualism, according to Andrews, consumerism coupled with sociopolitical and economic racism and alienation, MTV has become the latest "nanny" to surrogate and discipline some of our children. The refusal to adopt the practice of "generational-communication" has led to sociocultural and psychological isolation for this generation of black youths. What is "generational-communication"? It is the passing on of narratives and experiences for the purpose of self-preservation and instruction. In this context, the preacher to the black community or black leader must understand their role as continuous with the historical responsibility to instruct the community as others before him or her who did function as teachers, spiritual leaders, and social advocates and who brought awareness to the community.

The critical response calls upon every minister, especially those ministering to members of the black community to pay careful attention to what is happening to this present generation of black men. The high rate of incarceration of black men in this twenty-first century is symptomatic of deeper problems affecting the black youth. We are faced with the potential scarcity of black men to uphold the black family structure in America as the statistics reveal. With over 1.3 million black men detained and incarcerated, who will provide care and serve as a father figure for the little boys and girls? Yet some of these boys and girls sit in the pews of our churches. They are in our Sunday school classes. But the question is, will they still be there for them to develop the capacity to make the right decisions for life based on what they have been taught if the process of instruction is not intentional? With poor quality education and poorly resourced public school systems in the black communities, our attention should also be drawn to the pervasiveness of thug-life as a major challenge to urban black youths. According to Kenneth D. Johnson, the socioeconomic and political consequences and impact on the future of black youths is regrettable. He argues that

> structural changes in the economy demanding higher levels of education as the minimum passport for entry to gainful employment has left a generation of youths and young male adults behind . . . Due to broken families . . . increasingly young urban families, yield themselves to negative male peer influences in a desperate search for identity, security, and instruction on how to survive and get one's needs met in a hostile society. The previous buffering effects of the trinity of home, school and church have

been dissolved, with none of these institutions offering credible and engaging alternative lifestyle on a consistent basis that meet youth's needs for material security and advancement and to satisfy their need to belong to something greater than themselves. Thug life offers youths a seductive, but ultimately self-defeating set of choices that eventually result in harm.[175]

According to the Gospels, Jesus fed the hungry, conversed with the Samaritan woman, raised Lazarus from the dead, delivered the demon possessed man, fed five thousand people, healed the woman with the issue of blood, turned the tables upside down in the temple, rebuked the members of the Sanhedrin Council for their self-interest leadership and distortion of the Word of God, etc. Based on what Jesus did especially in light of things that negated the traditional perception, we find no distinction with respect to what was spiritual and what was social. God is calling us to be proactive by initiating evangelistic practices geared toward a holistic form of salvation that pursues the excellence of both spiritual and social transformation. The present situation of black men in America puts a burden upon churches and ministries, especially in the black community to begin to expand our concept of ministry. To the extent to which we seek to categorize and demarcate the teachings of Jesus Christ, it is to that extent to which we miss out on what God is saying to us. It is to that extent to which we constantly strive to domesticate God and identify God the Father, God the Son, and God the Holy Spirit with our individual self-interest and insatiable appetite for wealth and control to the detriment of those who need God's immediate intervention. But to the extent to which we allow the consciousness of God's redemptive activity to convict us and open our eyes to the plight of those around us, it is to that extent to which we can be saved and not resist the impetus to hear the groaning of this generation of black men. The critical response challenges the nature of our message and ministry.

The tendency to uncritically subscribe to the "prosperity" message is problematic in this regard. Preaching prosperity without a sociopolitical and economic analysis is equally compatible with preaching the Gospel of Jesus while avoiding the passages about Jesus ridding the temple of money changers, get-rich-quick preaching and preachers, racism in the Church,

---

[175.] *Antioch Agenda: Essays On The Restorative Church In Honor of Orlando E. Costas*, 2007, 214.

unscrupulous loan agents, etc. The logic of the prosperity message can be reduced to the following: if you are poor, it's because you have sinned or are living in sin, if you are rich, it's because God loves you and you are living a holy life. Poverty and the poor are associated with immorality and incontinence while wealth and the wealthy are associated with holiness and morality. As a result of this understanding of the Scripture, we excuse ourselves from helping and taking the initiative to help the poor, the marginalized and disenfranchised since it is their fault because of their immoral and sinful lifestyles. While I do believe the biblical injunction that the "wages of sin is death" (Romans 6:23) I also believe that there are social factors responsible for poverty and economic disparities. It is called "social sin." The prosperity message in its unqualified form distorts the nature of God because it becomes overbearingly judgmental and guilt ridden. If we biblically and logically analyze the argument for the popular prosperity teaching, we can conclude that all the poor people in the world are living in sin and out of God's will and that the over 1 million black men detained and incarcerated are there because they have sinned, are criminals, illegal, and untouchables. While there are some that are rightly detained and incarcerated, there are multitude of them who were arbitrarily and unjustly arrested and incarcerated to make up the detention and incarceration statistics and the quota for the support of the economic activities of the commercial prison—industrial complex. A proper elaboration of the prosperity message should be reflected in the preacher's desire to help those who are poor, sick, imprisoned, and widowed. Let them experience prosperity and not condemnation. The Body of Christ and the black community in this time need a holistic approach to ministry defined within the proper context of the gospel message of Jesus Christ.

A Pragmatic Response

The role of the Body of Christ in the world is both spiritual and social. It is on the one hand faced with the inescapable necessity to proclaim the spiritual message of Jesus Christ made possible through his shared blood on Calvary's cross. On the other hand, it is faced with the mandate to critique the sociopolitical and economic policies of the world in light of the socioeconomic plight of its people. It is the synthesis of these two responsibilities that are holistic, life transforming, and socially relevant.

The preacher of the gospel cannot afford to swing to one extreme and abandon the other but must hold both extremes together to derive a holistic ministry. The preaching of a "social" message and a "spiritual" message are in tension if the preacher sees the necessity of the social mandate of the gospel as undermining his Sunday morning sermon. Instead, the preacher on Sunday morning or during Bible study must allow the spirituality of his message and the mystical influence of the gospel to inform his social concerns and sensitivity, or the lack thereof—a synthesis that is not often of the head but of the heart as influenced by the Holy Spirit.

In this context, a pragmatic response is a tangible, realistic, and able-to-manage program that provides solutions to the high rate of incarcerated and detained black men, their struggling wives, and children. Any pragmatic program must have within its goals a focus on prioritizing the black family and focus on the men's ministry with the goal to intentionally foster a sense of personal development, self-responsibility and self-confidence. This intentional action should include prioritizing education and the development of skills. It means deconstructing the internalized stereotype that higher education and intellectualism is a white man's purview. Such ideas are rooted in the provision of poor quality education in the public schools in black communities and racism in the academy. On the other hand, others have gone through the crucible of rejection and despair in their desire to acquire higher education, and we can also make it if we are determined to break through the barriers at all cost. It implies that the Church and its leadership, the community and its leadership, are together called upon to inspire black youths to pursue both spiritual excellence and academic excellence. The following initiatives are suggested in light of the many good initiatives suggested in The Covenant With Black America.

1. Communicate with your children:

> Tell your children and your youth department members about the dangers of going to prison. Tell them: With a criminal record: they will experience economic hardship: it will be difficult to find employment, difficult to get a loan for college, almost impossible to purchase a home and because of the above, it will be almost impossible to properly take care of a family. And these hardships are to a large extent because of your criminal record. With a criminal record: you will be socially stigmatized and economically marginalized from mainstream society because of your lack of adequate education, joblessness and lack of skills for social mobility. As a result of this social marginalization, you

might end up going back to prison. With a criminal record, you are economically disempowered, politically you cannot vote and psychologically you will be very disturbed. Finally, in prison, people easily get infected with HIV and AIDS as a result of consensual and non-consensual sex between inmates than among people on the outside. In prisons, the use of condoms is not mandatory nor are they distributed. It is a hard life to live.

2. The establishment of church-based reintegration programs especially for juvenile ex-offenders:

Churches can participate in the intentional construction of programs to reintegrate ex-convicts with the hope of reducing the recidivism rate of black youths. A church-based reintegration program will make it possible for a smooth transition transition into the society for those released from prison.

3. The establishment of church-based programs for job training and job placement:

A church-based initiative for job training will make it possible for ex-offenders to get their GED, develop self-confidence, and not be ashamed of themselves. One of the major reasons for the high rate of recidivism among black men is the lack of education and skills needed for employment. As Bell beautifully articulates in his essay in *The Covenant with Black America*, the goal is "education rather than incarceration."[176] The focus should therefore be on improving quality education for black youths. The link between education and incarceration is reflected in the high rate of recidivism and prior incarceration record. Uneducated black men easily end up in jail because of the lack of skills for employment. The implication is that increase in the rate of high school dropout for black youths if not attended to with concerted effort, will eventually lead to more incarcerated black men in the commercial prison—industrial complex.

[176.] The *Covenant With Black America, 2006,* 65

4. The establishment of church-based Christian rehabilitation programs that caters to the black child's sense of consciousness made possible through the opening of Christian Restoration Homes:

> In this regard, churches can investigate the possibility of preventing black children from entering the Department of Youth Service (DYS) at the alarming rate at which it has been taking place. The ethos of the church based Christian rehabilitation program is its emphasis on rehabilitation and restoration through religious counseling programs rather than medication and seclusion. The goal is to prevent black youths from becoming perpetual inmates and addicts hooked on prescriptive drugs provided as a result of clinical measures. In this context, the Church is called upon to be proactive in employing the transformative understanding of the gospel of Jesus Christ.

5. The establishment of church-based Social Justice Ministry:

> Every church should endeavor to have a social justice ministry. The goal of this ministry is to inform and engage the church in issues of social concerns affecting the community. It means working in collaboration with other para-church organizations to be conversant and cognizant of the prevailing social conditions of the community.

The church that is serious about adopting the above points among others should know that it is taking a great risk. It will transform the ministry of the church in light of its commitment to the gospel of Jesus Christ. The church that wants to commit to the above must find rest in the fact that it is engaged in the proclamation of the pure gospel of Jesus Christ. On the other hand, if a church's focus is amassing wealth, simply increasing membership without committing to the social existential angst of its members, and the collaborative pursuit of spiritual and social consciousness as a holistic thrust of the gospel of Jesus Christ, it is missing out on meeting the full requirement of the gospel of Jesus Christ as found in the Scripture. Silence is the best weapon for normalizing a dangerous situation and insensitivity is its advocate.

Prayer

I confess, my God, that I have long been, and even now am, recalcitrant to the love of my neighbor. Just as much as I have derived intense joy in the superhuman delight of dissolving myself and losing myself in the souls for which I was destined by the mysterious affinities of human love, so I have always felt an inborn hostility to, and closed myself to, the common run of those whom you tell me to love. I find no difficulty in integrating into my inward life everything above and beneath me . . . But "the other man," my God—by which I do not mean "the poor, the halt, the lame and the sick," but "the other" quite simply as "other," the one who seems to exist independently of me because his universe seems closed to mine, and who seems to shatter the unity and the silence of the world for me—would I be sincere if I did not confess that my instinctive reaction is to rebuff him? And that the mere thought of entering into spiritual communication with him disgusts me?

Grant, O God, that the light of your countenance may shine for me in the life of that "other." The irresistible light of your eyes shining the depth of things has already guided me towards all the work I must accomplish, and all the difficulties I must pass through. Grant that I may see you, even and above all, in the souls of my brothers, at their most personal, and most true, and most distant.

You want me to be drawn towards "the other," not by simple personal sympathy, but by what is much higher: the united affinities of a world for itself and of that world for God.

You do not ask for the psychologically impossible—since what I am asked to cherish in the vast and unknown crowd is never anything save one and the same personal being which is yours.

Nor do you call for any hypocritical protestations of love for my neighbor, because—since my heart cannot reach your person except at the depths of all that is most individually and concretely personal in every "other"—it is to the "other" himself, and not some vague entity around him, that my charity is addressed.

No, you do not ask anything false or unattainable of me. You merely, through your revelation and your grace, force what is most human in me to become conscious of itself at last. Humanity was sleeping—it is still sleeping. A tremendous spiritual power is slumbering in the depths of your multitude, which will manifest itself only when we have learnt to break down the barriers of our egoism and, by a fundamental recasting of our outlook, raise ourselves up to the habitual and practical vision of universal realities.

Jesus, Saviour of human of activity of which you have given meaning, Saviour of human suffering to which you have given living value, be also the Saviour of human unity; compel us to discard our pettiness and to venture forth, resting upon you, into the uncharted ocean of charity." (Pierre Teilhard De Chardin, *The Divine Milieu: An Essay on the Interior Life*, 145-156)

Appendix

America Has Lost a Generation of Black Boys

By: Phillip Jackson
posted March 21, 2007 in the **Chattanoogan.Com**

There is no longer a need for dire predictions, hand-wringing, or apprehension about losing a generation of Black boys. It is too late. In education, employment, economics, incarceration, health, housing, and parenting, we have lost a generation of young Black men. The question that remains is will we lose the next two or three generations, or possibly every generation of Black boys hereafter to the streets, negative media, gangs, drugs, poor education, unemployment, father absence, crime, violence and death.

Most young Black men in the United States don't graduate from high school. Only 35% of Black male students graduated from high school in Chicago and only 26% in New York City, according to a 2006 report by The Schott Foundation for Public Education. Only a few Black boys who finish high school actually attend college, and of those few Black boys who enter college, nationally, only 22% of them finish college.

Young Black male students have the worst grades, the lowest test scores, and the highest dropout rates of all students in the country. When these young Black men don't succeed in school, they are much more likely to succeed in the nation's criminal justice and penitentiary system. And it was discovered recently that even when a young Black man graduates from a U.S. college, there is a good chance that he is from Africa, the Caribbean or Europe, and not the United States.

Black men in prison in America have become as American as apple pie. There are more Black men in prisons and jails in the United States (about 1.1 million) than there are Black men incarcerated in the rest of the world combined. This criminalization process now starts in elementary schools with Black male children as young as six and seven years old being arrested in staggering numbers according to a 2005 report, Education on Lockdown by the Advancement Project.

The rest of the world is watching and following the lead of America. Other countries including England, Canada, Jamaica, Brazil and South Africa are adopting American social policies that encourage the incarceration and destruction of young Black men. This is leading to a world-wide catastrophe. But still, there is no adequate response from the American or global Black community.

Worst of all is the passivity, neglect and disengagement of the Black community concerning the future of our Black boys. We do little while the future lives of Black boys are being destroyed in record numbers. The schools that Black boys attend prepare them with skills that will make them obsolete before, and if, they graduate. In a strange and perverse way, the Black community, itself, has started to wage a kind of war against young Black men and has become part of this destructive process.

Who are young Black women going to marry? Who is going to build and maintain the economies of Black communities? Who is going to anchor strong families in the Black community? Who will young Black boys emulate as they grow into men? Where is the outrage of the Black community at the destruction of its Black boys? Where are the plans and the supportive actions to change this? Is this the beginning of the end of the Black people in America?

The list of those who have failed young Black men includes our government, our foundations, our schools, our media, our Black churches, our Black leaders, and even our parents. Ironically, experts say that the solutions to the problems of young Black men are simple and relatively inexpensive, but they may not be easy, practical or popular. It is not that we lack solutions as much as it is that we lack the will to implement these solutions to save Black boys. It seems that government is willing to pay billions of dollars to lock up young Black men, rather than the millions it would take to prepare them to become viable contributors and valued members of our society.

Please consider these simple goals that can lead to solutions for fixing the problems of young Black men:

Short term

1) Teach all Black boys to read at grade level by the third grade and to embrace education
2) Provide positive role models for Black boys
3) Create a stable home environment for Black boys that includes contact with their fathers
4) Ensure that Black boys have a strong spiritual base
5) Control the negative media influences on Black boys
6) Teach Black boys to respect all girls and women

Long term

1) Invest as much money in educating Black boys as in locking up Black men
2) Help connect Black boys to a positive vision of themselves in the future
3) Create high expectations and help Black boys live into those high expectations
4) Build a positive peer culture for Black boys
5) Teach Black boys self-discipline, culture and history
6) Teach Black boys and the communities in which they live to embrace education and life-long learning

More Facts

- 37.7% of Black men in the United States are not working (2006 Joint Economic Committee Study chaired by Senator Charles E. Schumer (D-NY))
- 58% of Black boys in the United States do not graduate from high school (2006 Report from the Schott Foundation for Public Education)

- Almost 70% of Black children are born into female, single parent households (2000 Census Report)
- About 1 million Black men in the United States are in prison (U.S. Justice Department)

Phillip Jackson
Executive Director of the Black Star Project
Chicago, Il.
blackstar1000@ameritech.net

Bibliography

American Sociological Review, 2004, Vol. 69 (April: 151-169), Mass_
Imprisonment_and_the _lif . . . e_Race_and_Class_Ineq[1].pdf

Andrews, Dale. *Practical Theology For Black Churches: Bridging Black
Theology and African American Folk Religion.* Louisville: Westminster
John Knox Press, 2002.

Antioch Agenda. Eds. Daniel Jeyaraj, Robert W. Pazmino, and Rodney

L. Petersen. New Delhi: Indian Society for the Promotion of Christian
Knowledge, 2007.

Booth, Edward. *Saint Augustine and the Western Tradition of Self-Knowing.*
Philadelphia: Villanova University Press, 1989.

Bourke, Vernon J. *The Essential Augustine.* Indiana: Hackett Publishing
Company 1974.

Bowne, Parker Borden. *Theory of Thought and Knowledge.* New York:
Harper & Brothers Publishers, 1897.

Bowne, Parker, Borden. *Personalism.* Norwood MA: The Plimpton
Press, 1908.

Brown, Peter. *Augustine of Hippo*. Los Angeles: University of California Press, 1967.

Brightman, Edgar S., Moral Laws (New York: The Abingdon Press, 1933)

Brightman, Edgar S. *Person and Reality*. Ed. Peter A. Bertocci. New York: Ronald Press, 1958.

Brightman, Edgar S. *The Spiritual Life*. New York: Abingdon Press, 1942.

Brightman, E.S. Ed. *Personalism in Theology: Essay in Honor of Albert C. Knudson*. Boston: Boston University Press, 1943.

Burnell, Peter. *The Augustinian Person*. Washington, D.C.: The Catholic University of America Press, 2005.

Burrow, Rufus Jr. *Personalism: A Critical Introduction*. Missouri: Chalice Press, 1999.

Clark, Mary. *Augustine of Hippo: Selected Writings*. New York: Paulist Press, 1984.

Criminal Justice: Race and Criminal Justice, in *Compact for Racial Justice: An Agenda for Fairness and United* (A proactive plan for fairness and unity in our communities, politics, the economy and the law, Applied Research Center) rd_compact_fi nal.pdf, 17

De Chardin, Pierre Teilhard. *The Divine Milieu: An Essay on the Interior Life*. New York: Harper & Row, 1957.

Dickey, Laurence, and H.B. Nisbet, Eds. *Hegel, G. W. F. Political Writings*. Cambridge: Cambridge University, 1999.

Douglas, Kelly Brown. W*hat's Faith Got to Do With It*. New York: Orbis Book, 2005.

Du Bois, W. E. B. *Darkwater: Voice From Within the Veil*. New York: Schocken Book, 1969.

Du Bois, W.E. B. *The Souls of Black Folk.* New York: Dover Publications, Inc. 1994

Foster, Charles. *Black Religious Experience: Conversation on Double Consciousness and The work of Grant Shockley.* Nashville: Abingdon, 2003.

Fr. Thomas McGovern, *The Christian Anthropology of John Paul 11: An Overview* (www.Christendom-awake.org/pages/mcgovern/chrisanthro.htm.)

Fux, Pierre-Yves. *Augustinus Afer: Saint Augustin: africanité et universalité, Actes du colloque international Algers-Annaba, 17 avril 200.* Suisse : Editions Universitaires Fribourg Suisse, 2003.

Harrison, Carol. *Augustine: Christian Truth and Fractured Humanity.* Oxford: Oxford University Press, 2000.

Hegel, G.W.F. *Phenomenology of Spirit.* Translated by A. V. Miller. New York: Oxford University Press, 1977.

Hegel, Georg Wilhelm Friedrich. *Lectures on the Philosophy of World History.* Translated by H.B. Nisbet. New York: Cambridge University Press, 1975.

Hegel, G.W.F. *Elements of the Philosophy of Right.* Translated by Allen

W. Wood and H. B. Nisbet. Cambridge: Cambridge University Press, 1991.

Huntington, Samuel P. *The Clash of Civilization and the Remaking of the World Order.* New York: Simon & Schuster, 1997.

Jones, Whitney. *Basic Writings of Saint Augustine.* New York: Random House Publishers, 1948.

Johnson, Ben Campbell. *Rethinking Evangelism: A Theological Approach.* Philadelphia: The Westminister Press, 1987.

John Paul 11, *The Task of the World Culture of Today Is to Promote the Civilization of Love* (3 April 1987) no. 4, in English language weekly edition of L'Osservatore Romano 4 May 1987.

Karberg, Jennifer C., and Beck, Allen J. *"Trends in U.S. Correctional Populations: Findings from the Bureau of Justice Statistics."* Presented at the National Committee on Community Corrections Meeting, Washington, DC, April 16, 2004.

Kehr, Marguerite Witmer. *The Doctrine of the Self in St. Augustine and in Descartes* The Philosophical Review, Vol. 25, No. 4 (Jul., 1916), pp. 587-615.

Kirkham, Donald Henry. *"Pamphlet Opposition to the Rise of Methodism: The Eighteenth-Century English Evangelical Revival Under Attack,"* (PhD, diss., Duke University, 1973, p. 202) 21: 333

Lewis, David Levering. *W.E.B. Du Bois: Biography of a Race 1868-1919,* New York: Henry Holt and Company, 1993

Lewis, David Levering, *W.E.B. Du Bois: The Fight for Equality and the American Century:* 1919-1963. New York: Henry Holt and Company, 2000

Lubac, Henri de. *Augustinianism and Modern Theology.* New York: The Crossroad Publishing Company, 2000.

Sociology of Religion pg. 241. 2002, 63: 2 239-253

Marshall, Christopher D. *Beyond Retribution: A New Testament Vision for Justice, Crime and Punishment.* Michigan: William B. Eerdmans Publishing Company 2001

Marshall, Christopher D. *Prison, Prisoners and the Bible* (A paper delivered to *"Breaking Down the Walls Conference,"* Tukua Nga Here Kia Marama Ai, Matamata, 14-16 June, 2002 [Accessed. Feb. 2, 2009)

Marc Mauer, *Racial Impact Statements as a Means of Reducing Unwarranted Sentencing Disparities,* rd_racialimpactstatements.pdf, 22, Accessed 01/31/09.

Fr. Thomas McGovern. *The Christian Anthropology of John Paul 11: An Overview www.Christendom-awake.org/pages/mcgovern/chrisanthro.htm*

Vatican Council 11, *Gaudium et Spes* (GS) (*The Church in the Modern World*, 1965) and *Dignitatis Humanae* (Decree on Religious Freedom, 1965). 22.

Meagher, Robert E. *An Introduction to Augustine.* New York, New York University Press, 1978.

Nash, Ronald H. *The light of the mind: St. Augustine's Theory of Knowledge.* Kentucky: The University Press of Kentucky, 1969.

Neuhouser, Frederick. *Foundation of Hegel's Social Theory: Actualizing Freedom.* London: Harvard University Press, 2000.

O'Connell, Robert J. *St. Augustine's Early Theory of Man, AD 386-391.* Massachusetts: The Belknap Press of Harvard University Press, 1968.

Portalie, Eugene. *A Guide To The Thought of Saint Augustine.* Chicago: Henry Regnery Company 1960)

Rawls, John. *The Law of Peoples: with "The Idea of Public Reason Revisited.* London, Harvard University Press, 2002.

Rawls, John. *Justice as Fairness: A Restatement.* New Delhi, Universal, Low Publishing Co. Pvt. Ltd. 2001.

Rawls, John. *Political Liberalism* (New York, Columbia University Press, 2005),

Rizer, Arthur L. 111, *The Race Effect On Wrongful Convictions*: Rizer Article formatted Current. Doc, 7_Rizer[1].pdf, William Mitchell Law Review, Vol. 29:3 p 848. (Susan H. Bitensky, Section 1983: *Agent of Peace or Vehicle of Violence Against Children,* 54 OKLA. L. Rev. 333, 372 n.61 (2001); Constance R. LeSage, *The Death Penalty for Rape-Cruel and Unusual Punishment?,* 38 LA. L. Rev. 868, 870 n.8 (1978).

Russell, Robert P. *Saint Augustine and the Augustinian Tradition.* Philadelphia: Villanova University Press, 1970.

Saint Augustine: *Confessions.* Trans. Henry Chadwick, Oxford: Oxford University Press, 1991.

Saint Augustine: *The City of God.* Trans. Marcus Dods, New York: The Modern Library, 1993.

Saint Augustine: *The Trinity.* (*De Trinitate*) A.D. 400-416; PL 42, 8191098; trans. Marcus Dods, vol. V11.

Saint Augustine: *The Teacher* (*De Magistro*) A.D. 389; PL, 32, 1193-1220; trans. G. C. Leckie.

Saint Augustine: *Soliloquies,* 11 (*Soliloquia*) AD 387; PL 32, 869-904; trans. Nicene, vol. V11 (1888); Marcus Dods, reprinted in Oates, 1, 259-297; FOC 5 (1948); LCC 6 (1953). (

Saint Augustine: *Answers to Seven Questions for Simplicianus,* (*De diversis quaestionibus V11 ad Simplicianum*) AD 396-367; PL 40, 101-148; LCC 6 (1953), trans. V. J. Bourke

Saint Augustine: *On Musi., V1. 5: 12-13* (De *Musica*) AD 387-391; PL 32, 1081-1194; trans. FOC 4 (1947); Bk. V1 only, T. P. Mahar, S. J., St. Louis U. Thesis, 1939.

Saint Augustine: *On the True Religio., (De vera religione*) AD 389-391; PL 34, 121-172; trans C.A. Hangartner, S.J., *De vera religione* (Chapters 1-17) St. Louis University Master's Thesis, 1945.

Stock, Brian. *After Augustine: The Meditative Reader and the Text.* Philadelphia: University of Pennsylvania Press, 2001.

Stone, Ronald. *John Wesley's Life & Ethics.* Nashville: Abingdon Press 2001)

Sundquist, Eric, J. Ed., *W.E.B. Du Bois Reader.* Oxford: Oxford University Press, 1996.

The Covenant with Black America. Chicago: Third World Press, 2006.

The Methodist Review 1897 (http://docsouth.unc.edu/church/bowen/bio.html)

Thomas Jefferson, *"Notes on the State of Virginia,"* in *The Life and Selected Writings of Thomas Jefferson,* ed. Adrienne Koch and William Peden. New York: Modern Library, 1998.

Tillich, Paul. *Systematic Theology. Vol. one.* London: The University of Chicago Press, 1951.

Thurman, Howard. *With Head and Heart: The Autobiography of Howard Thurman.* New York: Harcourt Brace & Company, 1979.

Vatican Council 11. *Gaudium et Spes* (GS) (The Church in the Modern World, 1965) and *Dignitatis Humanae* (Decree on Religious Freedom, 1965).

Wesley, John. *The Works of John Wesley.* Ed. Richard P. Heitzenrater, *The Bicentennial Edition,* vol. 21. Nashville, Tennessee: Abingdon Press, 1992.

Wesley, John. *The Works of John Wesley.* Richard P. Heitzenrater, *The Bicentennial Edition,* vol. 19. Nashvill, Tennessee: Abingdon Press, 1990

Wesley, John. *The Works of John Wesley.* Richard P. Heitzenrater, *The Bicentennial Edition,* vol. 20. Nashvill, Tennessee: Abingdon Press, 1991.

West, Cornel, *Race Matters.* New York: Vintage Books, 2001.

Wilmore, Gayraud S. *Black Religion and Black Radicalism: An Interpretation of the Religious History of Afro-American People.* New York: Orbis Books, 1994.

Wittgenstein, Ludwig. *Blue and Brown Books.* USA: Harper and Row Publishers, 1958

Wogaman, J. Philip (Ed). *Communitarian Ethics: Later Writings of Walter*

G. Muelder. (Maine: The Preachers' Aid Society of New England in cooperation with BW press, 2007.

Zuckerman, Phil. Ed. *The Social Theory of W.E.B. Du Bois.* California: Pine Forge Press, 2004.

www.familiesoffreedom.org April 2, 2008

http://docsouth.unc.edu/church/bowen/bio.html

http://www.duboisle.org/html/DuBoisBio.html

www.sentencingproject.org/pdfs/brownboard.pdf, the Sentencing Project.")

http://www.ojp.usdoj.gov/bjs/pub/pdf/wo.pdf.

(*http://gbgm-umc.org/mission_programs/mcr/4.35/theprison.cfm*

http://www.hrw.org/reports/2001/prison/report.html

http://www.ussc.gov/crack/execsum.pdf

http://www.sentencingproject.org

http://www.heritage.org

http://www.sentencingproject.org/NewsDetails.aspx?NewsID=454

http://www.sentencingproject.org/NewsDetails.aspx?NewsID=454

www.Sentencingproject.org/rd_brownvboard[1].pdf

www.Sentencingproject.org/rd_brownvboard[1].pdf

www.Sentencingproject.org/rd_brownvboard[1].pdf

www.Sentencingproject.org/rd_brownvboard[1].pdf

www.Sentencingproject.org/rd_brownvboard[1].pdf

rd_crisisoftheyoung[1].pdf

http://www.latimes.com/news/local/la-me-nolan5ju105,

http://www.hrw.org/reports/2000/usa/Rcedrg00-01.htm

www. sentencingproject.org/women_cjs_overview(1)[1].pdf

rd_stateratesofi ncbyraceandethnicity[1].pdf

rd_stateratesofi ncbyraceandethnicity[1].pdf

www.Sentencingproject.org/rd_brownvboard[1].pdf,

www.Sentencingproject.org/rd_brownvboard[1].pdf,

http://www.abcnews.go.com/pringt?

http://www.beyond-the-illusion.com/files/issues/condom.txt

http://www.seattlepi.nwsource.com/local/300173_prison18.html

www.washingtonpost.com/wp-dyn/content/story/02/28/ST2008022803016.html.

Index

A

African Americans 40, 42, 44, 48, 55-6, 58-60, 64, 66, 102, 110, 112, 114-5
AIDS (acquired immunodeficiency syndrome) 15, 112, 116, 127, 133-4
Allen, Fred 35
Andrews, Dale 112
assimilation 34-5
Aufheben 19, 22
Aufhebung 18, 20, 74
Augustine, Saint 96-101, 105, 108, 148-9, 151-2

B

Bell, James 43-4
Black Church 7, 17, 24, 50, 98, 110-16, 118-19, 132
and Missionary churches 110, 116
Body of Christ 15, 24, 50-1, 116, 132, 137
Brooks, Thom 48

C

Christian Restoration Homes 140
concentrated poverty 61, 112

Conservation of Races, The (Du Bois) 105-6
Covenant with Black America, The (Williams) 43
criminalization 15-16, 18, 22-3, 39, 48, 53, 61-3, 81, 89-90, 96, 110, 121-2, 128, 144
critical response 121, 134-6

D

decriminalization 23
deferred enforced departure 29
Department of Homeland Security 23, 38
Department of Youth Service 60, 69, 140
double consciousness 106-7, 113, 149
Du Bois, W. E. B.
Conservation of Races 105
DYS *see* Department of Youth Service

E

economic dependency 62
economic marginalization 62, 64, 93, 127
Edelman, Marian Wright 43
Elements of the Philosophy of Right (Hegel) 16

F

Fernandez, Aida 35
freedom 21, 29, 33, 36, 67, 73, 76,
    79, 83-4, 90, 102, 114

G

generational-communication 135

H

Hegel, G. W. F.
   Elements of the Philosophy of Rights 18
Hoole, Joseph 130
Human Rights Watch 38, 48-50, 116

I

ICE (Immigration and Customs
   Enforcement) 38
imprisonment 7, 22, 43, 49, 56, 60-3,
   67-70, 76-7, 79-84, 131
incarceration 13-17, 39-45, 50, 53-4,
   57-60, 64-5, 67-8, 84, 89-90, 110,
   116, 120, 127-8, 132-5, 139, 143-4
injustice 53, 77, 83, 103, 124-6

J

John Paul II, Pope 14, 65, 102-4, 149
Johnson, Ben
   *Rethinking Evangelism: A Theological
   Approach* 117
Johnson, Kenneth D. 135

K

King, Martin Luther 45

L

Liberia 29, 31
life imprisonment 56
long-term imprisonment 81

M

Marshall, Christopher 14, 48
Mauer, Marc 42, 44, 59, 64, 150

McCall, Emmanuel 113
Methodists 130-2
Morgan, William 129, 132
Muelder, Walter G. 45, 154

N

New England Annual Conference 36, 40
nihilism 115-6
Nolan, Pat 56
Nopper, Tamara kil Ja Kim 46-7

O

On the Trinity 97
ontological distortion 84, 89, 93,
   121-2, 127
Oxford Methodists 129-30

P

persons-in-community 45
Peters, Sarah 129
Petersen, Rodney L. 13, 51, 147
Pew Charitable Trust 41, 54
poverty 24, 60-1, 70-1, 73, 82-3, 103, 137
   concentrated 61, 112
prison conditions 129
prison ministry 129, 132
prison population 44, 51, 58, 64-5, 76-7
proactive prayer 126-7
proactive praying 126
prophetic preaching 118
punishment 16, 18-23, 51, 63, 70, 73-
   5, 77, 79-81, 95, 127, 132, 150-1
   role of 22

Q

quality education 44, 60-1, 122, 135, 138

R

racial disparity 13, 53, 59-60, 123
racial justice 46
racial particularities 70, 121-3
racialization 17, 39, 48, 51, 62, 76,
   90, 95, 100, 107, 109

racism   14, 16-17, 23, 43, 51-2, 62,
    72-3, 81, 98, 100, 103, 107, 109,
    112-13, 135-6, 138
rational response   121, 128, 132
recidivism   39, 126, 134, 139
restorative justice   46, 51
*Rethinking Evangelism: A Theological
    Approach* (Johnson)   24
Rochester, New York   25

S

salvation   25, 41, 84, 94, 98, 113-14,
    118, 131, 136
scriptural holiness   131
self-deception   73
self-destruction   69, 73
self-distortion   73, 109
selfhood   89, 95, 99-100, 115
Sentencing Project   42, 44, 52-3, 55-6,
    59, 65, 68, 127, 154
sexual abuse, male prisoner-on-
    prisoner   48
Shockley, Grant   114
social holiness   131
social sin   137
Statement of Purpose   43
Syracuse, New York   25

T

temporary protective status   29
Thie, Brad   132
Toledo University   25
Trans Atlantic Slaver Trade   131
transparent engagement   127-8

U

United Methodist Church   36, 40
United States   13, 16, 18, 23-4, 28-9,
    31-3, 38, 41-2, 44, 48, 54, 58, 76,
    110, 133, 143-6

W

Weaver, Peter   35
Wesley, John   104, 129, 131, 153
Williams, Terry Tempest
    Covenant with Black America, The   43
Wimmer, Larry   35